Margaret Parry has combined a university teaching career in French literature, language and intercultural communication with her own personal writing. Her long-time retreat in rural France (le Perche) has been a great stimulus to her writing, including the present book. She initiated there, 'Les Rencontres de la Cerisaie', largely devoted to contemporary Russian writing, including that of the novelist and French academician, Andreï Makine, and in that context translated a life of the late Russian priest and martyr, Alexander Men. A specialist on François Mauriac, on whom she has published substantial articles in both English and French, she was a founder member in 1987, following the completion of her PhD, of the Association Européenne François Mauriac, which today has members in 18 countries and has published over twenty books on a range of contemporary European writers. Her most recent publication, *The War Poets and The Diary of an Ordinary Tommy*, based on the war diary of her grandfather, includes some of her own poetry inspired by two pilgrimages to the Somme. The author lives in Wensleydale, North Yorkshire.

For Joe

Margaret Parry

YOUR FACE MY LIGHT: MAURICE ZUNDEL, THE GOSPEL OF MAN

AUSTIN MACAULEY PUBLISHERS™

LONDON · CAMBRIDGE · NEW YORK · SHARJAH

A CIP catalogue record for this title is available from the British Library.

ISBN 9781528918596 (Paperback)
ISBN 9781528962377 (ePub e-book)

www.austinmacauley.com

First Published (2020)
Austin Macauley Publishers Ltd
25 Canada Square
Canary Wharf
London
E14 5LQ

Acknowledgements

I wish to thank, first and foremost, Revd David Wood, for his unwavering support and encouragement during the writing of this book; also, Philippe Labrusse, for his insight and knowledge on the question of translations of Zundel's work, as too for acting as intermediary with Père Bernard de Boissière, whose communication with me during his last illness was such an inspiration; my thanks to Anne Sigier, for her belief in my project and the insights she gave me into the publishing world; and to Père Michel Evdokimov, a light always in the background. I am also indebted to Marc Donzé, president of the Fondation Maurice Zundel, for his comprehensive authorisation, on behalf of the Foundation, to translate and publish extracts from Zundel's work.

God's presence can only become real in history, *our history*, through our mediation. He will appear in fact only to the extent that we let Him appear through us. It is useless to seek to demonstrate His truth with words; it is a question of manifesting His presence. His life is in our hands.

(*I is another*, p.59).

Contents

Preface

Maurice Zundel has a significant following in France as a spiritual teacher and writer but is virtually unknown elsewhere. This is a pity since he has much to say on the dilemma of the church in the Western world and because he developed a spirituality that can appeal across confessional boundaries. Margaret Parry has done a service in translating extracts from his work and introducing the main outlines of his life and thought to the English-speaking world.

For most of his life, Zundel was a marginal figure in the Catholic world, denied the kind of parish role that he really wanted. It may be that the authorities found his sympathies too wide for the usual ecclesiastical boundaries. However, in 1972, towards the end of his life, he was asked to lead a month-long retreat in the Vatican before Pope Paul VI and the curia.

Zundel remained a devout Catholic but was looked on with suspicion by the authorities for most of his life because his faith was able to embrace sympathetically those who found traditional statements of Christianity repressive. Certain protestant influences from his childhood and adolescence remained an active force in his life, shaping a more open, ecumenical vision. As a result of his long ministry in Egypt and the Lebanon, he was also able to include certain forms of Islam in this wide spiritual embrace.

Zundel believed we have to begin, not with the idea of a divine ruler but with ourselves and the question of what it is to be truly human. This involves coming to know ourselves and the person we can come to be through the way of dispossession. This includes cherishing the creative spirit within us and its sustaining source beyond ourselves. Like St

Augustine he had a strong sense of the beauty of God and wanted us to see something of that beauty in the face of others.

Essentially a person of prayer and spiritual guide, he always had an eye to the socially transformative effects of personal illumination. His wide sympathies, sense of the sacred and stress on the interiority of true religion will resonate with many today.

Richard Harries (Lord Harries of Pentregarth)
Former Bishop of Oxford

Prologue

Over the years the files had mounted on my desk, the name Zundel written on the spine…Zundel…ever again Zundel, an indication of the relentless urge to write something. As I made my jottings, page after page of them, did I ever consider what? I cannot remember. But then, all at once, titles began to emerge, a sign that something was taking shape, the rapidity with which they replaced each other, however, still denoting confusion – 'Maurice Zundel, Poet of the Invisible'… 'Maurice Zundel, the Reprobate Humanist'… 'Maurice Zundel: to the Unknown God'… 'Maurice Zundel, a New Apologia for the Faith'…

So the years passed, interrupted at times by different projects. But always I returned to Zundel. Like a persistent lover, he would not let me go. My own impulsion became ever more pressing. Then, one day, having read all of his books by now, from the flux within an idea crystallised. Through selected extracts from his work I would attempt a work of synthesis which would abstract the essence of his theology and of the man, the two interdependent. It would be in French, for long my preferred language of expression; an ardent interculturalist, I was drawn towards language as a way into the mindset of the elective 'other'. Who, in any case, except for a handful of readers in England, would have heard of Zundel?

Then the light dawned. Wasn't that precisely the point? Wasn't the English-speaking world, or a substantial section of it, as ready to be inspired, enlightened by Zundel as the sceptic you had once been? You might not see yourself as a translator at heart, but that surely was where the opening lay, this in the light of the general demise of faith, of churches closing by the week, of rampant materialism undermining traditional values and communal practices, of conflicting religious ideologies dislodging any basis of belief, in man let alone God. At the same time, more positively, there was the rising tide of 'spirituality', for many an alternative to faith if not a core adjunct of it. And there, surely, lay the great appeal of Zundel for those who shy away from dogma and formal religious beliefs and practices.

For in spite of things the religious instinct remains, perhaps strengthened as in past ages of crisis by the forces which rise in opposition to it, a reaction more imperative than ever at the present time, it would seem, in the light of the world forum at Davos of January 2018, which prompted one highly esteemed international commentator to reflect that never has civilisation come closer to extinction. So there emerge those rare individuals – 'les grands hommes' as the French refer to them – who respond to the moment and summon all their powers of thinking and feeling, and, in the silence of their hearts, cry 'stop, think further; all is not lost. Look into yourself; look into your fellows; the way is still open'. In the case of Zundel, from this silence a language is born which articulates this deep abiding instinct to others, a language still clothed in poetry and mystery, yet consonant with a post-enlightenment age of reason and human scientific thinking. If Zundel can speak so effectively to individuals in crisis (the testimonies are many from the French-speaking world), how much more, in his provocations, to a church in crisis? Maurice Zundel, an apologist of the new, a prophet, a mystic for our time…

Where, then, should I start? I thought of my own introduction to Zundel several years previously: after an exhilarating cycle ride over the plain one morning to the monastery of *La Trappe*, the chance reading in the bookshop there, lured as I had been by the title, of *I is another (Je est un autre),* which had been the start of my itinerary. Yet *I is another* is a late work, and as regards its core theme and the way it is developed, was not the most logical choice for a first reading of Zundel. No, *The Interior Gospel (L'Evangile intérieur)* which I had come to next would surely be a better choice. A much earlier work – Zundel's second in fact – it was short, easy to read, wide-ranging in its content, yet it homed in on the central theme of his theology: interiority. Based, moreover, on a series of talks given on Radio Luxembourg, it was addressed to a general public, not primarily a church-going public; one detects at times, in fact, a distinct note of sympathy for the reluctant believer.

The choice made, I launched into the translation. I soon found that it would not do at all. The translation (or as much as I had done of it) was stilted, unnatural; it did not render the voice I was looking for. Revisions followed but the impression remained. My enthusiasm diminished with the sense of my own inadequacy. The project was overtaken by others, in particular a venture into contemporary Russian writing, which took me to Russia and a face-to-face encounter with the iconic splendour of its churches. Hardly could I have realised how the one experience would feed into the other. When I returned to Zundel, for it was inevitable that I would, the title that caught my eye, undoubtedly through a trick of involuntary memory, was *Your Face my Light (Ton visage ma lumière),*[1] evocative of all those faces I had seen illuminated from within in the resplendent golden domed churches of Russia I had visited. The book, composed by the great specialist and luminary on Zundel, Père Bernard de Boissière, was a collection of Zundel's sermons delivered over the years in diverse countries and locations. As I read it, in short doses

---

[1] *Ton visage ma lumière, 90 sermons de Maurice Zundel*, Paris, Desclée de Brouwer, 2006, compiled by Bernard de Boissière. Bernard de Boissière was also co-author, with France-Marie Chauvelot, of the first authoritative biography of Zundel, *Maurice Zundel,* Paris, Presses de la Renaissance, 2004, to which I am indebted for many of the factual biographical details in Part I. On a personal note, I corresponded with père Bernard when my first manuscript was nearing completion. Sadly, he died shortly afterwards. I shall not forget the warm, generous nature of his response and his enthusiasm to see parts of *Your Face my Light* translated into English.

for it was that sort of book, I felt myself engaged in a living dialogue concerning the crisis of faith and of the church in today's world, listening to a voice attuned to the harsh realities of the world but at the same time speaking words, a presence not of this world.

The project was alive again. The book would be based on a selection of these sermons which reflected the essence of Zundel's theology as it developed over time, chosen especially to appeal to contemporary-minded readers, both those firm in the faith but also those struggling with belief or who had difficulty identifying with the church in its present form. For Zundel is essentially a writer for modernity. He serves Christianity in the modern age by adapting it to postmodern perspectives of individually perceived truth and freedom from dogma. A man of immense learning and culture, his theology is informed by the arts and the sciences, by philosophy and psychology. He sought new ways of tapping into the inner person and, in a society riddled with cynicism, scepticism and unbelief, of releasing the faculty of wonder before God's creation, an all-embracing notion with him… God's creation which, perhaps more fundamentally, he viewed as man's creation. Personal creativity was for him a moral imperative, the keystone of his theology.

Sermons – an already outmoded term, it has to be acknowledged – are not perhaps the most likely mode of expression to beguile new readers. Yet they have particular advantages for the translator, especially when it is a question of crossing cultures, offering perhaps a greater latitude than had been my experience translating *The Interior Gospel*. Sermons are spoken, thus in theory at least, are a more direct, more natural, more immediate mode of expression; and the author, in theory at least, has to find the right words from the start to convey understanding. He has not the same scope as the writer for elaboration (and sometimes obfuscation) as the latter gets carried away by his pen in the solitary act of creation. Yet it is true too that he can gauge immediately, through facial expressions, the degree of comprehension of his listeners, and amend, simplify, as the occasion requires.

The resulting rewording or repetition – for such it often is – perhaps sanctions a greater freedom on the part of the translator transposing from the spoken to the written word, where economy and precision still remain the order of the day. This is especially the case with Zundel who was often lyrical, even trance-like in his delivery. There is sometimes the need to amend, to tone down, even to commit the heresy of re-writing for a sentence or two so as not to offend an English ear, accustomed to a greater reserve as well as to a lesser degree of abstraction in religious expression.

On the latter question, however, artistic license is less of a temptation. Zundel created a new, an original theology. He needed a new language to express that theology. If he was largely bound by existing words, he used them in new ways, conferred on them new meanings and connotations, the subtleties of which, especially where there is word play as, for example, in his use of the words 'don' and 'donné', may be initially disorientating to an unpractised ear. Here Zundel's original terms have been retained, for they *are* Zundel, the core language of his living, breathing spirit. The 'prefabricated self', being 'source, origin and creator', 'self-dispossession' and 'disappropriation', 'inner space', the 'person', 'giving' and 'the given': the recurrence of these terms – and there are others – is such that familiarity is soon established, creating for us, too, a new language, which ideally extends the bounds of our own spiritual perceptions and understanding and capacity to know God.

This, essentially, is why I have wished to compose this book, aware at the same time that Zundel is not a writer to appeal to everyone. Zundel was a revolutionary – yet so was Christ – challenging traditional ways of thinking about belief. Some may not like his resistance to the God of the Old Testament. Whilst not ignoring the Fall and the story of God's chosen people, Zundel largely turns away from the Old Testament to focus on the splendour of Christ's coming to redeem man, opening up humanity to a new stage in its History, which embraces the idea of freedom. This would explain why Zundel talks about man as being at the beginning of History rather than close to the Last Days, revealing at this new dawn a changed topology of God and man, the latter endowed with the spiritual capacity to 'become God', to know true intimacy with Him.[2]

It was undoubtedly this spiritual unorthodoxy which troubled many in the Church establishment and left Zundel in a marginal position. To many lay people, however, tired of outmoded doctrines and attitudes and of paying lip service to a Church which continued to feed its flock on the 'milk' of St Paul rather than bringing its teaching and organisation into line with a changed human consciousness, Zundel represents the 'meat' of modernity. His theology of 'interiority', whilst based on the message of the Gospels, takes into account twentieth century explorations into the mind and the unconscious, into philosophy, psychology, literature and the arts, as well as the predominating values of freedom and responsibility. On the question of the arts generally and music in particular, which for many in today's world have become a substitute for faith, Zundel viewed them as being at the very core of faith, a manifestation of the creative spirit in man and affirmation of his divine nature, of man born in the image of his Creator. Today, forty-five years after his death, Zundel is no longer alone amongst prominent church leaders in suggesting that the Church can ignore at its peril the creative spirit in man collaborating, in Zundelian terms, with God to carry Creation towards its completion.[3] Yet at the same time as this opening in depth into new aspects of the human psyche, Zundel, in his simplicity of living and unending charity and outpouring of love, preserves intact the essence of Christ's model as transmitted through the Gospels. Despite, or because of, his unorthodoxy, Zundel today has an immense readership,

---

[2] He frequently cites St Augustine's statement: 'God became man so that man might become God'.

[3] Cf. Richard Harries, former bishop of Oxford, on BBC 'Thought for the Day', Feb/March 2015. See also, for example, Richard Harries, *Art and the Beauty of God*, Mowbray, 1993.

latest estimates indicating that the demand for his books continues to increase.[4]

Zundel, then, is a compelling writer. He is especially so for a linguist who has spent the entirety of a career exploring the mysterious edges of language and communication. Language as a concept is at the heart of Zundel's thinking. His passion was communication, relationships, based especially, however, on what is not said rather than on what is said, on what defies words but may pass in a look or a gesture, a far more effective means of apostleship to Zundel than talking about God. Some of Zundel's interlocutors had difficulty dealing with his long silences. Relationships transcended for him ordinary, everyday forms of expression. Yet his transfigured moments or 'heures étoilées', as he called them, could occur in the most ordinary of circumstances, for example watching a peasant woman engaged in the simple act of buying bread. Such is the mystery of human communication. It is not only a St Augustine or St Francis – Zundel's great heroes – who can point one beyond the veil...

Zundel makes life rich with possibilities and with the allurement of the unspoken, the silent. 'Silence' will be a recurrent theme in the sermons chosen below. These constitute Part II, the core section of the book. No introduction to Zundel, however, would be complete without a biographical overview of the man and his extraordinary life. This will be the subject of Part I and will situate, in passing, his key writings as the backdrop to his sermons or homilies, as the term will tend to be used.

---

[4] Information provided by the then president of the Zundel association (AMZ France), Philippe Labrusse, Paris, 2015.

Part I
A Life: Becoming 'Source, Origin and Creator'

(i) Childhood and Formative Influences: A Divided Inheritance

It was perhaps inevitable that Maurice Zundel should never entirely succeed within the Catholic Church, even if today his books are amongst the most prolific in the religious sections of bookshops in France and the French-speaking world and new Zundel groups are springing up regularly.[5] A newcomer to Zundel would find it hard to credit that despite his profound religious fervour and orthodox devotion to central articles of the faith – has anyone written more movingly about the Virgin Birth, about the Trinity, about the beauty of the Mass? – despite his brilliant mind and immense learning (he had a library of 3500 volumes) which he turned to the service of the church in both his preaching and the books he wrote; despite his saintliness and selflessness and human sympathy, which struck all of those with whom he came into contact…despite all of this, Zundel was during his lifetime essentially an exile, a marginal, much of his life spent as an itinerant mendicant preacher, without the personal parish he had so much longed for on ordination and in the years following.

The seeds of the problem and of the hostility soon felt by some within the church hierarchy to his difference or 'originality', as it came to be called, were undoubtedly sown in childhood, creating tensions in his nature between his deep-seated Catholicism and a propensity towards Protestantism. They derive in part from the town itself in which he was born. Neuchâtel in the Vaud region of Switzerland was, like much

---

[5] These are often small, intimate circles. The most recent one I heard about consists of only three persons, which produces its own home bulletin, one of several similar groups in the Paris region.

of the rest of the country, largely protestant. But since the middle of the nineteenth century a strong Catholic community had developed there, somewhat sequestered in its own part of the town and solidly ensconced in its traditions and observances. This was the milieu into which Maurice was born in 1897, into a family of well-heeled middle class respectability whose life revolved around strict Catholic observance, public service, and the education of its children. His father, Wilhelm, was a highly respected public administrator, founder and first president of the Catholic circle in Neuchâtel and an active member of various other Catholic institutions and charities. His uncle and godfather, Auguste, was also a devout Catholic, and a teacher in the Catholic primary school in Neuchâtel. Maurice was the third of four children – two sisters and a brother – and it was a secure, seemingly happy and close-knit family.

The atmosphere of piety and Catholic devotion and observance, combined with a natural religiosity in him, decided Maurice's vocation from an early age. Despite his strong academic interests and learning, which might have opened up any number of careers to him, the church as a vocation already dominated his mind and imagination. Following his first communion, he developed the habit of rising every morning at five to attend mass at the hospital chapel a half-hour's walk away – one of the foundations in which his father was active. It was served by a community of brethren whose black cassocks and white clerical collars clearly impressed him. He spent all of his spare time with the brothers and came to know their life intimately. They in their turn showed him great affection.

From his earliest childhood, however, there were other forces at work in him to complicate his vocation. Chief amongst these was his relationship with his maternal grandmother, who was a Protestant. Maurice was especially close to her and he soon came to recognise in her a form of religion different from that practised by the rest of the family. Whilst it is true that she had married a regular church-going Catholic who made it a binding condition of their marriage that their children should be brought up in the Catholic faith, she was sufficiently strong and independent-minded to remain true to her faith, yet with a discretion which raised no alarm bells as to the effect she might be having on her grandson. Maurice spent a great deal of time with her, accompanying her on her visits to the sick and needy. He warmed to her spontaneous sympathy and generosity, to her genuine, unforced love of her neighbour, to her reading of the scriptures which made of Christ a living person and presence. As time passed, he would come to cast a more critical eye on the religion practised by his milieu, which in comparison he would sum up as cold, formulaic, ritualistic, rich in words but poor on the Gospels, the living word of Christ. He would later describe his grandmother as 'the most Christian in the family', the person who had probably 'influenced him the most in life'.[6] Already in his early years a new form of Catholicism was taking shape in him, one in which openness of the heart and openness to the other and the sovereignty of the person took precedence over dogma, ritual and imposed belief.

As regards the religion of the heart his grandmother came to exemplify in his eyes, it is interesting to note too that she had lived for part of her life in Russia, together with her sister whose son had taken religious orders and become an Orthodox monk, a fact in which Zundel seems to have taken some pride. This strand, too, of his inheritance undoubtedly had some bearing on the development of his theology with its strong mystic, emotional and cosmic strain, as too on his natural sympathy with ecumenism. True to the Catholic faith as he remained and one of its most ardent apostles, he was also a man between religions. No small part of his attraction today is that his theology speaks between and across cultures, potentially at least, for translation remains an operative factor.

---

[6] De Boissière and Chauvelot, op.cit., pp.34-37, (my translation).

(ii) Schooling

As regards the presence of Protestantism in Zundel's early life, the influence of his grandmother, who died when he was ten, was maintained and reinforced by his schooling. It is perhaps surprising, given the strong division between Catholics and Protestants in Neuchâtel and the fact that his uncle taught in the Catholic primary school there, that his parents should have chosen to send him to the Protestant primary school. Academic factors undoubtedly weighed uppermost in their minds, the school in question providing a better preparation for the classical lycée, the automatic choice for a boy of Maurice's ability and calling, which would require a strong grounding in the classics.

The lycée had an excellent reputation and counted amongst its staff – all Protestants – a number of teachers of distinction. Distinction characterised too several of Zundel's contemporaries at the lycée who would themselves leave their mark on the world, amongst them the renowned child psychologist Jean Piaget. The humane, liberal, non-repressive atmosphere of the school and its respect for learning and for the intellect and individual personalities of its pupils guaranteed an environment in which talents and abilities flourished. Zundel was no exception and it says much for the school that, as the only Catholic in his group, he should have felt so much at home there. It says much too for the pupil Zundel himself, who already seems to have set his mind on the priesthood, that in his fourteenth year he should have been elected president of the school's thriving and highly esteemed science society, 'Les Amis de la Nature', where he developed a close network of relationships which would last through life. As president of the group he impressed his fellow pupils by his warm, welcoming nature, particularly to new members, a sign already of that attentiveness to the other which would distinguish him as a pastor and preacher. On the plane of scientific investigation itself and experience in the field, Zundel marked himself as different from his fellows, whose instinct was to rush in, to see, to touch, to analyse. He retained rather a position of detached reverence and contemplation, revealing already that propensity to inwardness and mysticism which would define all his relationships with phenomena, whether human or natural. He was already on the way to a spiritual understanding of science as an emanation of the divine truth, which would be such an important dimension of his theology.

A second important aspect of his lycée education was the learning of Latin, which gave him an enthusiasm and flair for languages to last through life. The school was well known for its revolutionary language teaching method – the 'direct' and 'applied' method, as the terms are used today. Latin was learned as a 'living', not a 'dead' language by situating it in a meaningful context – texts of human and historic interest which appealed directly to the intellect and imagination of the learners, a far cry from 'la plume de ma tante' approach. Live discussion of the texts themselves – a sort of total immersion – took precedence over the mechanics of grammar and rote vocabulary learning. Pupils apparently took to the method like ducks to water, achieving in one year a level of fluency achieved normally after five. The method appealed in particular to Zundel because it opened his mind too to the author of the text studied – the human subject behind words, the language used and the originator of them. He was already developing the habit of approaching the text as a living person. One can sense already why he would feel such a spontaneous affinity with the well-known French writer and critic, Charles Du Bos, a seminal figure in the Catholic revival in France, whom he would meet in Paris in the late Twenties, and why literature should assume such a central role in the development of his 'personalist' theology. Literature was a mode of interiority which took one to the essence of the person and a level of authentic communication. Like science, it was a manifestation of the divine truth. Zundel's classical education was humanist in the full sense of the word. It was not a question of Christianity or Humanism; they were twin sides of the same coin.

(iii) Moments of Grace:
A Vocation Confirmed

Three moments or epiphanies stand out in Zundel's early life which confirmed him in his vocation and determined the nature of his spiritual orientation. The first, akin to the transforming moment of revelation of a Pascal, or Claudel, or John Wesley, occurred when he was only fourteen in the red church – as it was called – at Neuchâtel. Kneeling before a statue of the Virgin of Lourdes, he suddenly experienced an influx of grace, a sense of deep and illuminating inward purity and space. It was essentially a revelation of the mystery of the Immaculate Conception, of the trinity of the Godhead incarnate in the Virgin, a figure of pure transparency and oblation. The moment was a decisive one in the conception it gave him of 'maternity' as transcending any idea of gender, and of the ineffable nature of relationships, deriving from the accessing of this virginal space (or 'creative void' as he would also come to refer to it), the prerequisite for true openness to and encounter with the other. His lyrical evocation of this moment in his second book, *The Interior Gospel (L'Evangile intérieur)*, is an indication of its transformative, mind-changing effect on him:

"What words can express the joy which flooded the adolescent's heart on coming face to face one day, in a mood of piety, with the tenderness of the Virgin? An image of woman is imprinted on his heart which nothing will ever efface. He sees her in the full force of her dignity, in the ineffable transparency of her inner life and the silent radiance of a redemptive purity. He understands, beyond anything words can express, that woman is spirit like man is spirit. Her true glory is within and one has to communicate with her soul in order to penetrate her mystery... The young man suddenly sees the world in an entirely new way: all is light, order and beauty."[7]

This first revelation was soon complemented by a second one, in which the focus was now Christ as a transcending figure of earthly love. If the experience was deeply Protestant in nature, the Gospel suddenly becoming for him a living, personal voice addressed directly to him, this is hardly surprising. For its agency was a young Protestant friend of his, an apprentice mechanic working-class boy whom he met regularly on an evening to discuss the Bible, religion, and literature, as well as more worldly social issues, especially working-class conditions. The experience occurred whilst listening to his friend reading the Sermon on the Mount to him. Zundel had by his own admission his first true revelation of the New Testament as a living reality, a 'divine friendship', a truth to be lived rather than listened to as part of a drily delivered doctrine which 'goes in at one ear and out at the other'. Zundel lost no time in decorating his room with the verses of the Beatitudes, describing the occasion in retrospect as 'the dawn of a religious life which resembles a movement of the spirit.'[8] One can sense already the importance of the title he chose for his second work, L'Evangile intérieur – for many people still his most popular work. These early moments of grace, to be supplemented shortly by others, in particular his encounter with St Augustine in the Confessions, confirmed Zundel on the path of interiorisation which became the cornerstone of his theology.

The Bible was not alone in bringing about a revolution in Zundel's heart. The episode of the Sermon on the Mount was complemented by another, again through the agency of his working-class friend, a devotee of literature but who had had to renounce his studies in order to earn a living. One episode

---

[7] Maurice Zundel, L'Evangile intérieur, Ed. St Augustin (8th edition), 2007, pp.56-57, (my translation).
[8] De Boissière and Chauvelot, op.cit., pp.45-46, (my translation).

stands out from their discussions on literature as providing him with a living example of the 'interior gospel'. It was the famous episode in Victor Hugo's novel *Les Misérables* when the abbé Myriel, full of Christ-like compassion and charity, conceals from the police the theft committed against him by his lodger, the convict Jean Valjean, and rehabilitates him in society, the latter now giving to the poor the money he earns from work. The episode brought home to Zundel not only the plight of the poor and marginalised which, through his encounter with St Francis – the most frequently recurring figure in his writings and reflections – shaped the central tenets of his spirituality. It brought home to him too the power and mystery of words as generated from within, from the depths of the writer's creative spirit, to work on people's minds and imaginations and liberate their deepest instincts of love and compassion. The Jean Valjean episode was one of the seminal moments of his life, which shaped his desire to be a priest of the poor.

(iv) Towards Ordination: Einsiedeln

There was one further revelatory experience of adolescence, not in this case single, instantaneous, but rather in the nature of a cumulative experience which worked on him day by day to elevate him to a regular plane of mystical contemplation. This was his encounter with the monastic life at Einsiedeln, the foremost monastery of Switzerland with its beautiful abbey church, and a high place of the Benedictine Order.[9] Did Zundel have higher motives than the desire to learn German in transferring there at sixteen, following an interim year at the training seminary in Fribourg where he had been required to complete a year's philosophy study? With its repressive, disciplinarian – and in a now Catholic context – anti-Modernist atmosphere, Fribourg must have come as something of a shock to Zundel after the liberal, stimulating atmosphere of the lycée at Neuchâtel. In the silent, contemplative and beautiful environment of Einsiedeln, he found himself again and the sense of his vocation crystallised.

Zundel's spiritual experience at Einsiedeln had a strong aesthetic dimension, participation in its daily observances giving him the inspiration for his first book, *The Poem of the Holy Liturgy (Le Poème de la sainte liturgie)* – the first word of his literary output ('poem') is one to be noticed – which, on publication (at first in the form of separate articles), would establish his early reputation and promise as a priest. Zundel was overwhelmed by the beauty of the abbey church and the liturgy, as by the beauty of soul of the abbot and the saintly

---

[9] See John Russell, *Switzerland,* Batsford, 1962, pp.143-153.

authority he exercised over the community, which after Fribourg he found so liberating. Though still pursuing his studies for the baccalauréat in preparation for the priesthood,[10] Zundel together with his fellow aspirants participated in the life of the community and wore the monk's habit. He attended high mass, vespers and compline daily, and the atmosphere of silence, meditation and inward focus had a profound effect on him. Not only did it lay the foundations of his life as a writer, but also he soon knew that the cloister was his calling and he became an oblate of the Benedictine Order.

The dream, however, was soon shattered by external events. In 1915, shortly after the outbreak of war, a new ruling was introduced, and as a French-speaking citizen Zundel was required to leave Einsiedeln, after only two years there. One can imagine his dejection on having to return to the stultifying atmosphere of the college at Fribourg. Yet though Zundel was effectively renouncing his dream of the monastic life, it is probably true to say that a part of him never entirely left Einsiedeln. It was surely of Einsiedeln he was thinking when he wrote in *The Interior Gospel*:

"Prayer carries one to those supreme heights of self-oblation in which the soul is lost in God and transfused into the stained glass of the cathedral through which His light shines down on the world. You probably ask yourself what purpose monasteries serve, and whether their inmates could not live a more useful life elsewhere. I would say 'No', for they fulfil the highest purpose that a free humanity can fulfil, which is to connect the material world to the Spirit."[11]

With his inwardness and worldly detachment – though, interestingly, he would later deny that he was an introspective by nature[12] – Zundel remained essentially a monk all his life,

---

[10] The chapter on Einsiedeln in Walter Weideli's book, *Moine aujourd'hui* (Ed. Du Cerf, 1986), gives a useful insight into the educative structures of the monastery.

[11] Op.cit., p.77, (my translation).

[12] *Itinéraire,* in *L'Homme passe l'homme, Itinéraire,* Ed.du Jubilé, 2005, p.523. (The book was written between 1939 and 1946. It was first published in 1948 by La Colombe, Ed.du Vieux Colombier.)

the many retreats he led across Europe and the Middle East, especially at the Carmelite convent of Matarieh in Cairo, undoubtedly providing the most fulfilling moments of his life.

One can only admire the way that, back in the college at Fribourg with its uncongenial, authoritative atmosphere of the Thomist revival and a pedagogy based on proving God by arid, rote-learned formulae and the technique of argument and counter-argument honed by practice, Zundel launched himself into his studies. He developed what became a life-long practice of working through the night, learning by heart in preparation for his final examination vast tracts of Aquinas's *Somme théologique (Summa theologiae)* with its core Catholic doctrine. Intent on not deviating, however, from his own individual course, he reserved the best part of the night for his own personal reading, study and writing. Zundel completed his studies with brilliant results two years ahead of his time. He would be the first Catholic priest since the Reformation to be consecrated in Neuchâtel.

(v) First Ministry, the Priest Errant: Geneva – Rome – Paris – London

Geneva (1919-1925)

Zundel was ordained priest in 1919. His appointment as vicaire to the largest parish in Geneva – St Joseph's – was a propitious start. It was a largely working-class parish and Zundel launched himself into his varied activities with great enthusiasm and zeal. In addition to his teaching and pastoral duties there was charity work, the hospital chaplaincy, catechism classes, religious classes with secondary school pupils, lectures to university groups, and the running of the Foyer, a sort of girls' 'Sunday cum day school' for working class girls in the parish. He wrote regular articles for newspapers and religious journals, whilst continuing his own personal reading and studies. His overfull schedule left little time for sleep, which he kept at bay with cigarettes: two packets a day became a life-long habit! Of his various activities, probably the one closest to his heart was the girls' Foyer which brought together fifty or so girls of varying ages and abilities from modest, often deprived backgrounds. He expended a great deal of energy and initiative on it, making of it a charity organisation of the highest order, creating at its centre a small chapel and elaborating a teaching programme aimed at the spiritual, intellectual and social development of his charges. His vision was all-embracing, focusing on the central articles of the faith, yes, but presented in such a way as to make real to them the idea of the 'living treasure' within their hearts and a sense of their own self-worth and dignity in the eyes of God. It was an ideal of personhood which depended for its attainment on the liberation of faculties repressed in many of the girls by the conditions into which they had been born. He sought to open their minds to the pleasure of books and painting and music, to foster the art of discussion and self-expression, and on a more down-to-earth plane to raise their awareness of everyday aspects of family life – hygiene, family relationships, relations with the opposite sex. Eyebrows were undoubtedly raised as word got around about his unconventional programme and methods. Suffice it to say that for many of the girls the Foyer was like a second home that compensated for fundamental wants in their immediate family. Some of the girls continued to correspond with Zundel for the rest of his life and testified to the transformative effect on them, socially and culturally, of his brief presence in their lives.

Zundel's engagement in all aspects of his life at St Joseph's was total. If his unorthodox approaches – in teaching the catechism too, and in his close familiarity with students whom he met out-of-hours to discuss political and social questions – were for long overlooked or tolerated, undoubtedly due to his burgeoning reputation as a preacher and theologian which brought honour to the parish, the situation suddenly changed. This was, following an important finance meeting in the parish, when he preached a sermon on the church of poverty, where he put forward the radical view that the church was failing in its mission if it sought to accumulate wealth rather than spending its yearly surplus on the poor. Out of the blue, Zundel received a letter from his bishop proposing a sabbatical at the papal university in Rome, the Angelicum (named after Il Angelico, Thomas Aquinas), to enable him to pursue his doctoral studies. Without any prior consultation Zundel was being distanced from the life he loved and which he must surely have felt was advancing him to his dream of a parish of his own, to take up residence at the very centre of Thomist theology, from which he felt himself more and more alienated. Dismayed, Zundel submitted to the will of his superiors and left for Rome. The six years he had spent in Geneva was the longest period he would spend in any appointment. Henceforth his life would essentially be that of a marginal, an itinerant. He was a man under surveillance, too unorthodox in his ways for a very orthodox church.

Rome (1925-1927)

The punishment of exile, if such it can be called, quickly transformed itself into an opportunity, a fairly typical occurrence at difficult moments in Zundel's life. In the congenial atmosphere of Rome where he was essentially his own man, Zundel rediscovered the joys of free intellectual enquiry. All the more so as the subject of his research – the influence of Nominalism on Christian thought – enabled him to delve more deeply into Thomism and to give a more intellectual basis, accommodating 'reason', to his own more subjective, mystical, intuitionist approach to divine knowing,

His already 'modernist', immanentist thinking was reinforced by what was probably the most momentous event in his life. This was his 'encounter', during a trip to Florence, with St Francis of Assisi.[13] What was the precise nature of the revelation? It was confrontation with the divine attribute of poverty – Dame Poverty as St Francis called her. The idea of poverty laid total claim to Zundel's mind, carrying him bit by bit far beyond the social significance of the term, however central to his vocation that remained, to acquire a deeper metaphysical meaning which he placed at the very centre of his 'personalist' theology.

A second key aspect of his stay in Italy, which worked in conjunction with the inspiration from St Francis and contributed to the development of his personal theology, was the overwhelming impact on him of its art and architecture. As his period at Einsiedeln has demonstrated, Zundel was no stranger to aestheticism, that is, to the spiritually awakening and transformative power of art. In Rome and Florence and their environs, the richness and diversity of such experiences

---

[13] It is interesting, as an example of cross-currents of experience between generations and cultures, to compare Zundel's encounter with St Francis with that of François Cheng in his recent book, *Assisi*, Albin Michel, 2015.

led him to meditate more deeply on their mystery and significance. The idea of the 'creative spirit' in man, encapsulating and capable of expressing the divine attributes of beauty, truth, goodness, and now poverty, evidence of man's closeness to the divine, of man born in the image of God the creator and thus, potentially at least, in a spiritual relationship with his fellows, assumed an ever greater place in his thinking. Aesthetic inspiration was a liberating of the person as 'source, origin and creator' – a phrase which occurs as a leitmotif in his writing – and as such a force for liberation of the other in a movement of altruism which he would define as one of 'circumincession' akin to the Trinity: God – the person – the other...a movement of spiritual transparency dependent, as will be seen as his thoughts crystallise, on a state of 'dispossession', or 'disappropriation' of the self; (he developed a whole panoply of terms to express the idea.)

Ideas were already fermenting in Zundel which would be central to his first book, *The Poem of the Holy Liturgy*. The significance of the first word in his literary output – 'poem' – is already becoming apparent. If it is a book about the beauties of the liturgy or Catholic mass, on one level purely informative as it outlines the different stages of the mass and their significance, at a deeper level it is a meditation on language and the incapacity of words to express the ineffable, a preoccupation undoubtedly deriving from his own experience whilst writing. Yet examples abound between the lines – from the psalms, from the liturgy itself, from poetry generally – which dispute his hypothesis. The key point is that whilst writing on the one hand in the pure church tradition of apologist for the faith, on the other he is engaged in a personal disputation about art, confronting head-on, from an orthodox perspective, the problem for right-thinking clergy of aestheticism, of man's capacity to know God by his own creative endeavours. If the book was generally well received on its first publication[14] – indeed it was used as a guide by

---

[14] This was a shortened version, published by Ed. St Augustin in 1926, based on articles he wrote during this period for the *Courrier de Genève*, of the final book published in 1934.

oblates at Einsiedeln and elsewhere – there were others who discerned in it a humanist tendency which might have a deleterious effect on its readers.

Zundel, then, by the end of his two-year period in Rome, despite having followed the path set out for him by his superiors and having successfully completed his doctorate, was still a subject of disquiet for certain hard line clergy back home, in particular for his bishop and mentor, Mgr Besson. Alert to any signs of apostasy in his diocese in the strained atmosphere between Catholics and Protestants, the latter judged it expedient to move Zundel yet again, at least in the immediate term, to Paris. One can imagine the effect of this decision on Zundel, eager after his two-year exile in Rome, whatever benefits it had provided, to return to his pastoral and preaching ministry in Geneva. Exile was surely looking like a form of banishment, unwarranted punishment for having an original and creative mind, when all he longed for was to return to his parishioners and seek to make ever more real to them, and to all he came into contact with, the love, the compassion, the presence of God in their lives, and in that quiet, undemonstrative, personable way which was his very nature.

Paris (1927-1929)

The machinations to keep Zundel at a safe distance from Geneva do not reflect well on his superiors. The harshness of his sentence is all the more apparent when one considers the nature of his new appointments, the first, in the summer of 1927, to assume general parish duties as a vacation replacement for a young curate in Paris. When this expired and, lost, humiliated, he refused the possibility of an extension, he was given a low-level appointment in the Paris suburb of Charenton. His duties there ranged from responsibility for wedding arrangements (essentially, no doubt, income generation in secular parlance) and at the other extreme arranging activities for the recalcitrant youth of the parish whose sole motivation seemed to be the football field.

Zundel's duties at Charenton could not have been further removed from his ministerial, pastoral and educational work at St Joseph's in Geneva, where he had felt his talents and capabilities utilised to the full. Literally dragged into the mud on a sometimes daily basis, Zundel sank into the depths of despair, describing his period there as his Cross, surely wondering if there could ever be a resurrection. Paris, the place of dreams for so many, was for him a place of downfall, of a punishment of the most demeaning kind, chosen by his cool-headed bishop as being more in keeping with his neurotic temperament than the tranquil terrain of Geneva. His only moments of light were the occasional trips he made into the centre of Paris on a weekend, instigated by a young priest he had met in Rome who had learned of his plight. Bit by bit, through the offices of this same friend, he developed a network of relationships which included some key figures in the Paris religious and literary world of the time – the abbé Altermann, well-known at this important period of the Catholic Revival in France for his conversion of a number of prominent writers (François Mauriac and Charles Du Bos, for example) and Jacques Maritain, famous for his Soirées de Meudon (Zundel had earlier attended one of his retreats at Meudon). It was through their intervention that a post was found and offered to Zundel commensurate with his education, intellect and calling.

The post in question was as a chaplain to the Benedictine Abbey of the rue Monsieur in Paris,[15] a community of about eighty nuns and one of the most prestigious religious centres in France, well-known throughout Europe for the people connected with it. It drew people from far and wide for the beauty of its sung liturgy – comparable to Solesmes – and for its deep atmosphere of silence and devotion. Amongst its habitués to daily mass were many figures from the Paris intelligentsia, prominent Catholic writers and members of the priesthood, certain of whom Zundel came to know well. Two

---

[15] The rue Monsieur Le Prince was commonly referred to in this context as the rue Monsieur.

in particular played an important role in his life, the abbé Montini, later to become Pope Paul VI, and the already mentioned anglophile writer and aesthete Charles Du Bos, to whom for a time Zundel served as confessor. Two of Zundel's books, to be referred to subsequently, were intimately connected with them: *Openings to truth (Ouvertures sur le vrai)* dedicated to the memory of Charles Du Bos, and his last work published posthumously *What man and what God (Quel homme et quel Dieu)* based on the retreat he preached at Pope Paul's invitation in the Vatican in 1972.

As regards the friendship with Du Bos, the atmosphere of the rue Monsieur, redolent of Einsiedeln, can only have precipitated a relationship based on a mutual attraction to the inner life as the way to true communication and Being, fostered in Du Bos's case by his Bergsonian, intuitionist approach to literature, and to be developed more fully as a theological concept by Zundel. There seems little doubt that Du Bos's spiritualist conception of literature ('the meeting-place of two souls'),[16] in terms of which the reader seeks a state of total coincidence with the writing subject – the 'real self' of the author – and to apprehend the creative impulse or inner necessity behind the work, focused or reinforced Zundel's interest in literature as a way into the Self (*le moi*) and to God, or the Presence (a more neutral word which he often uses in preference to God). In his short treatise on literature produced (initially) in 1938 shortly before his death, Du Bos described literature and art as an 'incarnation' of the Word: "In the Word was Life [he quotes] and the Life was the Light of men."[17] One can see the connection with Zundel's pithy chapter heading (reversing the words of St John) 'The Flesh made Word' in Zundel's first book *The Poem of the*

---

[16] Charles Du Bos, *Qu'est-ce que la littérature*, Lausanne, Ed. L'Age d'Homme, 1989, p.20. Du Bos's importance in the Catholic revival in the late Twenties in France is studied in detail in my doctoral dissertation, *Time and Consciousness in the Works of François Mauriac* (University of Leeds, 1985) – though I had not read Zundel at this stage!

[17] Op.cit., pp. 98-101, (my translation).

Holy Liturgy (1935) which deals so centrally with the question of art, and writing, and language, a heading which gave him some trouble with his superiors and his labelling by some as a humanist. One has only to wait for his lyrical discourses on St Augustine to see how far from the mark his detractors were and how lacking themselves in true spiritual discernment. Had not Augustine himself stated that 'God became man so that man might become God', a statement frequently quoted by Zundel and redolent of his own affirmation in his sermons, 'Heaven is here within you'?

As regards his other friend, the abbé Montini, the latter might still at this period be preaching a more conventional God high in his heaven alert to the sins of man. Four decades on, and now Pope Paul VI, it was the interior God of Zundel he was intent on promulgating, to this end inviting Zundel to preach the Vatican retreat referred to.

One further name to be retained from this decisive period in Zundel's life, this time in relation to his growing interest in ecumenism and to his later periods in Egypt and the Lebanon, is that of the renowned Oriental scholar, Louis Massignon, who opened him to the world of Islam.

There are undoubtedly other names worthy of mention. Sufficient has been said, however, to indicate that after the dark days of Charenton Zundel had indeed experienced his resurrection. It was a period when, by his own admission, quite apart from his official duties he had time to think and read, to delve deeper into his vast store of books, to attend lectures by the most prestigious speakers on the most wide-ranging subjects – not only religion and the arts but science, sociology, psychology. "In this heavenly place I started to live again," he states.[18] His spiritual and intellectual life was in full flow, bringing together the different strands of his thinking to form the basis of his own personal theology, which over the years he would elaborate. And this theology, a specialist study of these months spent with the Benedictines indicates, was already influencing not only those in the abbey

---

[18] De Boissière and Chauvelot, op.cit., p.165, (my translation).

itself but Catholic thinking generally.[19] But perhaps Zundel's own words best sum up the heady atmosphere of these months and the challenge they represented:

"I read a great deal during this period in Paris and was able to get up-to-date with all the debates that were in the air. This was the period when I broke with Thomism, when I sought to discern the truth as it came to me personally. Everything had to be changed, thrown into question – the whole of the Bible, of tradition, of the liturgy, of Christian morality, of philosophy, the entire conception of knowledge, because everything had to be made to pass from outside to inside. It had to move onto a completely different plane, the plane of total liberty."[20]

Zundel, then, felt himself on the brink of a revolution, one which today, however, almost a century later, has hardly made its mark in the way he surely dreamed of. Yet more and more people are reading Zundel, and it is perhaps a 'sign' of the relative nature of time in relation to great cultural shifts that the words quoted figure in that deeper more abstract work *L'Homme passe l'Homme* and *Itinéraire* which is a summa of his theology. Did Zundel aspire with this work to emulate, and indeed to surpass in terms of the revolution he dreamed of, St Thomas's *Somme théologique*? One can only speculate. The one thing that can be stated with certainty is that the preliminary to the 'itinerary' outlined in this book was the liberating months he spent at the Benedictine Abbey of the rue Monsieur, where he at last made his break with Thomism.

Zundel's life in the rue Monsieur was so rich, it left such a deep mark on him that one has the impression he spent several years there. In fact he was there for only eighteen months. Was it homesickness, the desire to be accepted back to Geneva and resume his work as a parish priest, so cancelling out the stigma of exile, which made him consult his superior Mgr Besson? Whatever information the latter

---

[19] Ibid.

[20] Quoted by Jean-Pierre Gay in *L'Homme passe l'Homme and Itinéraire*, op.cit.., p.8, (my translation).

may have received in the meantime regarding Zundel's growing reputation, he remained intransigent. Zundel was not yet ready to be received back into the fold.

Having made the break in his mind with Paris, Zundel asked to be considered for a posting in London. The motivation is unclear. Had his interest in England been aroused by his Anglophile friend Charles Du Bos, or by his personal interest in the Anglo-Catholic Cardinal Newman, or by the desire to come to a closer understanding of Anglicanism and acquire the rudiments of English as part of his leaning towards ecumenism? Probably it was a combination of all of these factors. At all events, Mgr Besson conceded to his wish.

So came to an end his brief period in Paris which, looking back on it, stands out almost as an act of providence reminiscent of turns of fortune in the life of certain patriarchs.[21] If, through the perversity of others, Zundel had not traversed the 'Cross' – or hell – of Charenton (the name itself an ironic reminder of the ferryman of the Styx), would he have found his resurrection via the rue Monsieur, to become the renowned writer and theologian we know, whilst never ceasing to be a pastor and preacher who like that apostate of Anglicanism, John Wesley, 'made the world his parish'. 'God moves in a mysterious way his wonders to perform', the well-known hymn reminds us. Zundel's life could so easily have gone in a different direction, his legacy have remained more indeterminate. Paris placed itself on his itinerary at just the right time… Paris, la ville-lumière, the city of light: from the murk of the Styx Zundel was being drawn to the radiance of the icon which, in *Itinéraire*, he defines in terms of an 'intentionality of the Other', a 'transcending altruism in which the spirit moves out towards the Light, offering itself to its radiance'.[22] From the perception of that distant glow, Zundel's life never deviated.

---

[21] Cf. Thomas Browne, *Religio Medici*, 1635, Everyman edition, p.27.

[22] Op.cit., p.532, (my translation). As regards the term 'Other' in this quotation, Zundel clarifies in this same work why he writes the

London (1929-1930)

After the light and clarity of Paris, the few months Zundel spent in London, from late 1929 to June 1930, emerge in comparison as a rather dusky, shadowy period, no doubt in keeping with the English climate and London fogs to which he would have been acclimatised by Du Bos. With only the rudiments of English at his disposal it must, initially at least, have been a period of loneliness. Yet as at other important moments of his life Zundel showed himself a man of purpose and focus. With that exemplary attitude towards languages, both ancient and modern, which accompanied him through life – how else come closer to the roots of cultures as suggesting to the mystic he already was not separateness, difference, the curse of Babel, but the universal reality transcending them ? – he was soon, with the help of a dictionary, working his way through the *Apologia* of Cardinal Newman: Newman, an Anglo-Catholic priest with whom he must have felt a particular affinity, persecuted as the latter had been by the orthodox hierarchy of his own church (interestingly, moreover – looking ahead in Zundel's case – neither of them receiving official consecration until into their seventies). By the time Zundel finished the work, he was sufficiently fluent in English to converse with his superior in the Assumptionist convent in Kensington where he was working as assistant chaplain, and with other Anglican priests he met, and to follow divine offices (whether at St Paul's, Westminster Abbey or local churches) as well as public lectures. Through one priest in particular he was introduced to a number of well-known bishops, facilitating admittance to major Anglican ceremonies and other events which interested him, particularly in the ecumenical movement; so he was able to extend his insights into divergences and commonalities of

---

word with the capital ('l'Autre'). In Zundelian theology the other person, that is the 'real self' as distinct from the 'biological self', is the ultimate agency of Self-knowledge, transcendence, liberation. L'Autre may also signify God, the divine 'Presence'. These concepts, as will be seen in Part II, figure frequently in his sermons.

religious understanding between Catholics and Protestants, Jews and Muslims. But it was through his experience of Anglicanism in particular, with its more liberal, pragmatic approach to ritual and dogma that he came to probe more deeply the nature of religious truth.[23] This, from the thirties on, became a major orientating force of his writings, all the more pressing to him no doubt in the light of his abandoning of Thomism. His subjectivism and personalism became ever more pronounced. As for his mystical fervour, this could only have been nourished, under the aegis of his literary mentor, Charles Du Bos, by his encounter with the English poets – Shelley, Keats, Coventry Patmore amongst others, whom he frequently cites. Zundel was plunged into the realm of nature and re-enchantment with the cadences and musicality of words to evoke the divine, which he had expressed so powerfully in his *Poem of the Holy Liturgy*. Characteristically, Zundel did not leave London without translating, for his own edification, extracts from the poets too!

---

[23] Cf. *Le Mystère de la connaissance* (*The Mystery of Knowing*), unpublished, 1932 ; *Ouvertures sur le vrai* (*Openings onto Truth*), completed 1939 with the dedicatory note, 'A la chère mémoire de mon ami Charles Du Bos, Bex (Suisse), 8 décembre 1939', Carmel de Matarieh, Le Caire, 29 janvier 1940; published posthumously by Desclée, 1989.

(vi) Itinerant Teacher, Preacher and Writer; Egypt, the War Years

Following London, Zundel's life settled into a fairly regular pattern of teaching, itinerant preaching and writing. In his early work as a parish priest in Geneva, Zundel had already demonstrated his flair and originality as a teacher of the young – of girls from a predominantly working-class background – which earned him life-long testimonies from some of his pupils and their parents. Over the next decade he had further similar appointments, but with girls now from the affluent middle classes. Zundel might have objected to his next appointment as chaplain at an international boarding school convent at Vevey on the shores of Lake Geneva, on the grounds that he was being treated as a student-priest, conscious that this was yet another move on the part of his superiors to keep him from the position of parish priest he was so much hoping for. He soon settled into his new work, however, devoting much of his energy and creative flair to re-writing the catechism currently in use, which fell far short of his ideal of religious instruction. His motivating principle as priest and teacher was not to transmit ready-made rules and dogma concerning God and the Christian life. It was to open the minds and the hearts, and the critical intelligence and imagination of his students, to encourage them to feel from within, to develop a sense of their inner being and to come of themselves to the big questions of life and religion and the sacrament of relationships, including those of the couple. One can imagine the attitude of some in the hierarchy to rumours of his approach. His new catechism was soon, however, being used covertly in parts of the diocese and, as the years passed, in religious communities more generally. It was eventually published in book form in the late forties under the title *Search for the Unknown God (Recherche du Dieu inconnu)*, and was recognised by Pope Paul VI in his later eulogies of Zundel as a book of true 'spiritual initiation'.

Whatever frustrations Zundel initially experienced at being in a post not to his choosing, he must have derived great satisfaction from watching the growing maturity of his students, with whom he had considerably more scope on an intellectual plane than with his earlier pupils in Geneva. He could not fail to have been aware of their enthusiasm for his approach and of their lasting appreciation. He left a spiritual legacy at Vevey, as would be the case with his next post four years later at a girls' lycée at Neuilly in Paris. Here too it was not only his teaching but also the experience of personal encounter with the man Zundel himself, whether in the classroom, at mass or at confession, which left their mark, extraordinarily on occasions when no words passed. However individual the testimonies, they are alike in conveying a sense of true spiritual encounter and communication (or communion). Such encounters were the source of many conversions and of an illuminating Presence which lasted through life.

Even if the Neuilly posting was not again what Zundel had initially hoped for, it must have been a period of great intellectual refreshment and renewal for him. Within the school itself as in the collège Sévigny where he took on additional duties, both schools known for their high academic reputation, not only was he working with staff of the highest intellectual calibre, enjoying a particularly close and stimulating relationship with the Principal. He was able to resume contact with those he had met at the Benedictine Abbey of the rue Monsieur. He was soon frequenting other intellectual circles and salons, where he met some of the foremost philosophical and religious thinkers of the day. However actively engaged Zundel continued to be as a priest – as his reputation spread there were more and more solicitations to give lectures and lead retreats, sometimes well beyond the Paris region – the nature and length of the appointment (approximately six years with the inclusion of a sabbatical) gave him greater opportunity for study, to consolidate his evolving theology, and to devote more time to writing. It was in the middle thirties, more or less half way through his posting at Neuilly, that he published what would probably be his most popular book, *The Interior Gospel (L'Evangile intérieur),* based on a series of talks aimed at the general public which he had been invited to give on Radio Luxembourg. The title itself points to the essence of Zundel's spirituality and theology – interiority – and indicates the profound influence on him of that other great saint, Augustine, author of the *Confessions.* Alongside St Francis he was arguably the greatest inspiration of his life, as his frequent quotations indicate, not the Augustine who believed in the elect of souls – such a concept of God was completely alien to Zundel – but the writer who so eloquently persuaded him of the reality of God's living presence within him, a presence transfused with Beauty which liberated the creative spirit in man. The interest in beauty, art, creativity, so essential a part of Zundel's theology and an aspect of his thinking which suggests his closeness to an Orthodox and Oriental mind-set, is already a central theme in *The Interior Gospel*, perhaps the best introduction to Zundel for the general reader.

Egypt, the War Years

Zundel remained at Neuilly until 1939 when, due to the outbreak of war, it was necessary for him to leave France. Still not welcome back to his home parish in Switzerland, Louis Massignon, the great Islamist scholar and friend of Zundel's from the rue Monsieur days already mentioned, suggested that he go to Egypt. During his period at Neuilly, Zundel had been granted the long-held wish of a sabbatical (1937-1938) to be spent at the Ecole Biblique in Jerusalem in order to study ancient languages, with a view to coming closer to the truth of biblical texts. His stay there had opened his mind in other ways. Ever alert to social and political injustice and oppression in the world, Zundel had found himself engaged in the question of Zionism and the ousting of Arabs from their homeland. Virtually an expatriate himself now, Zundel seized on the opportunity offered by Massignon. Through his network of contacts, the latter found him a chaplaincy appointment at the Carmelite Convent of Matarieh in the suburbs of Cairo. If anywhere was to be Zundel's home, it was surely here. The few months envisaged for his stay there stretched into seven years. Following that, moreover, from 1946 until the end of his life, whether he was based in the meantime in Switzerland or was travelling around Europe lecturing and leading retreats, he returned every two years to Egypt, as at regular intervals to the Lebanon (an 'adorable country', he stated) where he was welcomed with open arms at the Dominican Convent of Beyrouth.

The small community of nuns at Matarieh where, tradition has it, the Holy Family stopped on its journey to Egypt, was overwhelmed by Zundel's presence. Quite apart from his chaplaincy work there, through contacts like Massignon, he was soon actively engaged as a teacher and preacher in the intellectual and religious life of Cairo more generally: at the Conference Centre for Christianity and Islam, and more especially, in the Melchite Greek Catholic Community, considered to be the highest centre of religious learning in Cairo. He enjoyed excellent relations with the bishop and future patriarch, Mgr Hakim, who gave him responsibility for Catholic teaching in the College. He was also actively involved with scout and guide groups, to whom, it is to be noted, he dedicated his book *Itinerary (Itinéraire)* of 1947. He also had bi-monthly lecturing assignments in Alexandria.

Zundel's period in Egypt was a seminal one in his life, not only for the close friendships he developed there which sustained him throughout the rest of his life, and for his sense of belonging which must have made up for what he had lacked as an aspiring parish priest. It was important, too, for the knowledge and understanding he developed of Islam. Characteristically, he continued to learn Arabic so that he could read the Quran in the original. There was much that drew and fascinated him in the Islamic faith. Undoubtedly, he was drawn by the poetry of the Quran with its ever-present image of a garden running with living water, reminiscent of his own poetic rendering of Christ's encounter with the Samaritan woman, probably his most frequently recurring reference in the New Testament. He must have instinctively warmed to the mystical aura of the language itself and the use of chant, which accentuated the beauty of sound and evoked the ineffable in words more effectively, perhaps, than the Western transmission of scripture; as indicated earlier, the shortcomings of language as a medium of expression of the divine truth was a central preoccupation of Zundel in his first book, *The Poem of the Holy Liturgy*. The idea of the text as conveying a real Presence, intrinsic to the Quran, is fundamental in Zundel's writing, as will become increasingly evident.[24]

On a different plane, one can question whether Zundel interpreted too literally the Quran's emphasis on the clemency and mercy of the Islamic God, contrasting it with his own view – somewhat stereotyped – of the authoritarian, despotic God of the Old Testament high in his heaven separate from man, which, regrettably, seems to have prejudiced him against the Old Testament in general. Zundel was a theologian of the New Testament and curiously seems to have been able to accommodate Allah within his theology.

Zundel must also have been impressed by the way in which Islam was a living faith, an integral part of the people's cultural identity, of life as it was lived on a daily basis, with no apparent separation between the outer claims of living and the inner world of belief. Zundel may have remained a Catholic all his life, and of the most devout, exemplary kind, seeking through his preaching to give ever deeper understanding and meaning to the central articles of the faith. His Catholicism was nevertheless transfused with an inclusive, non-confessional spirituality which reaches to the

---

[24] For a fuller development of the question of language in the Quran, see Karen Armstrong, *Mohammed, a Biography of the Prophet*, chapter 6; Victor Gollancz, 1991.

very heart of man, of man conceived universally, seeking to know himself in his most intimate being. 'What is man?' The question preoccupied him more and more, as is reflected in the titles of both books and articles he wrote from the forties on: *Man surpasses man (L'Homme passe l'homme)*[25] (1944), *Do you believe in man? (Croyez-vous en l'homme?)* (1957), *Does man exist? (L'Homme existe-t-il?)* (1967). Man, it appears, takes precedence over God as his central subject...that is, until his final book, *What man and what God (Quel homme et quel Dieu)* (1976), where they figure side by side, of equal status. Or perhaps they are not equal, for the first question is of man, not God: how can man achieve his full status as Human? On probing into the question of human identity, arguably the core question on both a secular and religious plane in the later twentieth century and early twenty-first century (Zundel's reading embraced in particular the psycho-analytic field and he used the phrase 'psychology of the depths' in relation to his own spirituality), he must have sensed all that Catholicism and other confessions of the West had to gain from an understanding of the religions of the East.[26]

As has been indicated, during his years in Egypt Zundel was fully active both as teacher and intellectual as well as priest and preacher. His reputation grew rapidly and, after the ostracism of Switzerland, the high esteem accorded him must have been a great stimulus to his ongoing research and creativity. Zundel may have had his detractors, those who either did not understand or did not sympathise with his ideas, which were too unorthodox for them or too ahead of their time. The great majority of his followers, however, were magnified by his sermons and lectures which attracted people of every confession, young and old alike, as well as atheists,

---

[25] The different conventions for the use of capitals in the titles of French and English books sometimes makes it difficult to render in translation the full implications of words, or indeed to interpret them.

[26] Zundel was also interested in Buddhism and the Hindu faith and was an avid reader of Gandhi.

Marxists, and anarchists. Rumours of his success can hardly have pleased Mgr Besson who as recently as 1938 had agitated to have his book *Quest for the Person (Recherche de la personne)* put on the Index because of the chapter on the sexuality of the couple. Undeterred, and with no obstacle in his path now but time, for his working schedule was ever fuller, Zundel continued to read and study and follow the creative impulses of his inner life which yielded ever new perspectives on the central line of his theology. His mind was always broadening and deepening as he sought to keep up with new spheres of learning which might affect the psychology of modern man, the tragedy of Hiroshima, for example, leading him to books on mathematics and atomic science.

Zundel's rich intellectual life which recognised no limits to its creative possibilities was one aspect of the Cairo experience. At the other extreme was his religious asceticism. This was the period when he was brought face to face with poverty on a scale not previously experienced and when St Francis dominated his mind more and more as a model to emulate. Zundel had lived on charity for almost all of his life. It was now that he developed the reputation of a latter-day Il Poverello, giving away almost everything he received, whether monetary gifts, food, clothing, or other aids to daily subsistence to beggars in the street, retaining only the bare essentials for himself and living on a frugal diet of potatoes, saint-like bearing no grudge against the opportunists amongst the recipients of his charity who regularly queued up at his door for more.

'Le don' – giving: this was at the very core of Zundel's theology; but more than material giving it means 'self-giving'. This is a difficult, essentially metaphysical as well as mystical concept (if the latter are not contradictory terms). But no, the 'highest mysticism' for Zundel is precisely that 'which is most capable of transforming the real', of making possible the 'promotion' and 'advent of humanity'.[27] The 'self' in question is precisely that part of one's being which is most precious yet least accessible within oneself. It is one's essence or innermost 'originary' being, an emanation in Zundelian terms of the divine, creative source, thus God-like capable in a movement of Love of transmitting its light and truth and of liberating the same instinct of generosity and human sympathy in the 'other', in an endless chain of sympathy or inner communion. Zundel's theology is one of interrelationships, interpenetration, interpersonalism. Becoming a 'person' or 'someone' means achieving that state of being he calls the 'oblative self', which is an attainment of total transparency with oneself through giving up everything one is in material or 'social' terms[28] in order through what can only be called a human act of revelation to bring light to the 'other' and an inner encounter with the true self.

Living in accordance with the Gospels is thus in Zundel's theology a continuous act of self-domination, that is, of 'dispossession' or 'disappropriation' of one's outer 'social' self – all those attributes of one's nature such as pride, vanity, the maintenance of status and appearances in the eyes of the world, which distract one and act as a barrier to self-knowing and true spiritual being. Zundel was only too well aware of how challenging the gospel of Love, or Charity (as expressed in Corinthians), was, to be lived fully. Conscious of his own manifold failings – he lists for example amongst others his strong will and instinct to dominate – he knew how difficult it was to transform what he called the 'possessive' (or possessing) self' into the 'oblative self', and so attain the inwardly transformative love as exemplified by Christ, most strikingly in his encounter with the Samaritan woman.

Poverty, then, for Zundel, was essentially a spiritual attribute. It signified inwardness, the movement of interiority away from the noise and agitation of the surface being to a

---

[27] *Présence de Maurice Zundel*, bulletin of the Zundel Association (AMZ France), no.91, July 2015, p.7. (my translation).
[28] 'Social' in philosophical terms as meaning the opposite to the 'real'.

state of inner silence which, when fully realised – but who, except the saint and mystic achieves such a state – signified unity with God, God who embraces all men in Himself. Interiority, the central message, as has been seen, in his *Interior Gospel* of 1936, far from distancing oneself from the 'other', as might be initially supposed (an attitude inherent in criticism of monasticism as an institution), leads one into the heart of the other still waiting to know itself and the call to human perfection. 'What man...?' to resume Zundel's question cited above. The *Interior Gospel* leads him over the years, as his perceptions deepen, to the alluring title of *I is another*. Though not published until 1971, it is foreshadowed as a theme in much of his earlier writing, for example in his equally alluring title of *Man surpasses man*. Is there anything to stop man achieving his divinity? St Augustine's statement is never far from Zundel's mind: 'God became man so that man might become God'. 'Might become'... Man for Zundel remains, as will be seen, 'l'homme possible' – the possibility of man.

(vii) The Remaining Years; Consecration

Under the more liberal-minded successor of Mgr Besson – the latter died in 1945, the year prior to Zundel's return from Egypt – Zundel was at last offered the possibility of his own parish. He declined it. In so doing, whatever his reputation in Europe and the Middle East as preacher and theologian, as teacher and pastor to whom people flocked for confession and spiritual guidance, he was accepting a place in the Church hierarchy as 'auxiliary', and that for the rest of his life. But were titles of any account to Zundel? Were they not inseparably bound up in his mind with the idea of the ego, the world of appearances, the 'persona' which got in the way of the 'person', man's highest expression of himself? Zundel had probably come closer to this ideal of being or 'personhood' in Egypt and the Lebanon than at any previous period in his life.

Even though he returned to Switzerland in 1946 and the country served as a base for the rest of his life, he had lost his sense of roots there. Egypt was his home in the Biblical sense of a place of spiritual belonging. Whilst he remained ever faithful to Catholicism and was engaged to the full in the Church's efforts to adapt itself to the modern world, at the same time, through his encounters with Islam, Greek Orthodoxy and other confessions, he gravitated towards a Church which transcended frontiers, creeds and confessions. He was an 'apostle' in the true sense of the word, carrying the Word to 'the nations'. His intellectual life in the form of the books he wrote, facilitated by his greater freedom as an auxiliary, was an integral part of his apostolic activity, taking him ever deeper into the mystery of language itself as an instrument of divine intelligence.

If the key staging posts of these years were arguably the books he wrote, which carried him ever forward to greater spiritual and creative heights, his public life as a teacher and preacher was as full as it had ever been. These were crucial years in the history of the Catholic Church. The worker-priest movement initiated by the Dominicans, comparable in spirit to the Wesley movement in England two centuries earlier out of which came Methodism, forced the Church to confront the plight of the uneducated working masses and its responsibility towards them. Various papal encyclicals sought to define the Church's position in relation to the social and economic issues rapidly transforming the world and people's moral attitudes. Since his earliest years, Zundel had not ceased to be involved in social and political issues and to make his views public. In his later years, whilst his commitment remained undiminished, he now had his books to speak for him and to articulate his ideas more specifically in the framework of his own spirituality. This was especially so on the question of education – how, in the interests of 'personhood',[29] could the mind and the spirit be liberated in those for whom life was a relentless daily struggle to obtain the barest means of subsistence? – and on the ownership of property, justifiable in his view as signifying a 'space of security' enabling one to become 'a space of generosity' but questionable as a right when it was surplus to one's needs.[30] He was critical too of the proposed liturgical reforms concerning the end of the Latin mass and practice of Gregorian chant, so conducive in his view to that otherworldly atmosphere and experience of silence in which God's presence became manifest. He felt the very foundations of his theology threatened.

There were forces in the background, however, to save that theology, of which he could hardly have been aware. It is

---

[29] The question of 'personhood' will be developed in Part II, chapter 6.

[30] Ibid.

ironical that Zundel, who for so much of his life had been at odds with the Church hierarchy, should have his life and his career consecrated by the Pope himself and in the very centre of Christendom, Rome. One can imagine Zundel's astonishment when, after decades of surveillance and marginalisation by the Church, he received a letter from the Vatican inviting him to write a book on the Church and the present-day problems of the world. This was followed, in January 1972, by a further invitation from the Pope, this time to preach the Vatican retreat in Rome the following month, before the pontiff himself and the Curia.

Pope Paul VI, elected in 1963, was the same abbé Montigny whom Zundel had come to know well at the Benedictine Abbey of the rue Monsieur at the end of the twenties. He had been a part of the same intellectual and spiritual atmosphere imbued with Bergsonism and the idea of *devenir*, that is, the freedom of the human consciousness to participate in the spiritual creative force immanent in the world, carrying it towards its perfection. Though their paths had diverged, Montigny had followed Zundel's writings closely. He admired them for their spiritual depth and the authentic faith inspiring them, as too for their literary qualities and cultural depth. He recognised in Zundel a priest who could articulate better than any other the present-day problems of the world and open a way via the Church and its priesthood to the future of Man.

Did Paul VI presume too much of Zundel, who had only a month's notice to prepare the retreat, entailing four sessions per day over a week-long period in front of the cream of the Church hierarchy? It was a month already heavy with other teaching commitments both in Switzerland and France. Zundel arrived in Rome with next to no preparation, a situation which might have traumatised some; but Zundel was a man usually at ease with the extempore spoken word. He decided to base the retreat on his most recent book, *I is another*, which he felt was particularly apposite to the question of the crisis of the Church and the modern world. It would challenge his hearers to consider the question of their own personal perception of God and their relationship with Him, and how their faith as such operated in the world of men, in their personal relationship with others. Was God a truly interior God, as exemplified by St Augustine, who transcended persons in an all-embracing aspiration (and respiration) of unity, bringing man into an equal relationship with Him, the breath as it were of his breath, the spirit of his spirit? Or was He part of an external truth or reality, separate in nature and identity from man? Was the trinity but a beautiful metaphysical concept for the elevation of men's minds to contemplation of a mystery beyond themselves? Or was the trinity, via clergy and pastorate and practising believers, transferable to the level of man, instituting an order of relationships in which the 'person' was one in an intercommunion and becoming of Humanity?

The public homage paid by the Pope to Zundel following the retreat leaves no doubt as to its success and the Pope's personal satisfaction. Here at last, after a long and testing vocation, was Zundel's consecration as a great Church leader, an inspirer of minds and a liberator of souls. And it might surely be seen as a mark of God's providence and sign of Zundel's future glory, that at this supreme moment of his earthly existence he should have been brought to the Eternal City.

Who could have foreseen, however, that the Vatican retreat was to be Zundel's 'new' beginning or 're-naissance' in the sense he had used the word in relation to the story of Nicodemus, so central to his theology? The hard graft of preparing the text of his sessions for publication after the event was undoubtedly only one factor in his suddenly deteriorating health. The symptoms became ever more serious over the three years following. Zundel died in 1975 after a harrowing illness which, tragically, left him without the power of speech, words, which had been his supreme gift and grace in life.

What a crucifixion! It was as though, in death, Zundel had indeed become 'God made man', that Christ-like he had risen to the ultimate sacrifice of himself, the living Word. Was it

59

surprising if so many of his associates referred to him already as a saint? Zundel would have refused the term. He was a man like any other, Sisyphus-like pursuing the daily struggle of existence, each new day a new beginning.

In his immense modesty and humility lay Zundel's greatness as a man and his accessibility as a pastor, teacher and theologian, however mind-challenging some of his writings are. Intellectuals of his generation often reflected on their version of 'les grands hommes' – 'great men' – those who had left their mark on the world and on the progress of man. Certain of his contemporaries, indeed, devoted a whole book to the subject.[31] Zundel never wrote his book on St Augustine or St Francis, the two great inspirations of his life. He did not need to. His own life was an expression of them, a living text.

Zundel nevertheless left a scattering of aphorisms on the subject. This is probably my favourite, taken from his 1939 book *Openings onto truth (Ouvertures sur le vrai)* dedicated to his Anglophile friend, the writer, poet and aesthete, Charles Du Bos:

"Great men are those who restore us to silence and confront us with the light. Our borders retreat, an infinite space opens before us and we stand trembling on the doorstep of our own sanctuary."

It is time for Zundel's own words to speak for him – Words, or the impossible words he was always seeking for in the depths of his mind, from his first book to his last, those that would cast aside the veil...

---

[31] For example, François Mauriac, *Mes grands hommes*, Paris, Ed. du Rocher, 1949.

Part II
Words: An Apologia for Faith, from Virtual Man to Living Cathedral

Foreword

As indicated in the Prologue, the texts constituting Part II are translated extracts from the book of sermons collated by Père Bernard de Boissière under the title *Your Face My Light (Ton visage ma lumière)*. They are selected with a view to homing in on particular aspects of Zundel's theology and are arranged according to the developing nature of that theology. Some of the chapter headings are retained verbatim; others are modified in order to give greater prominence to the key theme(s) treated. Each chapter is introduced by a brief commentary by me (in italics) on the themes covered and to highlight the developing nature of Zundel's thinking. This is followed (in normal script) by a major section from one of the sermons in *Your Face My Light*, supplemented, in the final section of the chapter by shorter extracts, under the title 'Echoes and Reflexions: the Written Word', from a range of written as compared with oral texts, which serve to broaden the frame of reference. On a purely technical point, capitals are retained in the translation where they figure in the original.

Zundel's theology is attractive to some because, whilst assuming that everyone has a spiritual life, it does not automatically assume that everyone, even at times regular churchgoers, wishes to be addressed in the overtly religious language of Church teaching. Whilst it is true that large sections of Zundel's books discourse on the Bible and central articles of the Catholic – and Christian – faith, perhaps the most relevant and illuminating parts of his writings for some, in an age of unbelief which increasingly undermines people's sense of who they are and where they belong, are those dealing with spirituality more generally and as transcending the boundaries of any particular confession. Whilst the concept of a 'Presence' occurs repeatedly in his writings and will automatically signify to perhaps the majority of Christian readers the spirit of God within, Zundel frequently demonstrates that it can be interpreted in other ways too, indeed in any number of ways, according to the disposition and experience of the reader or listener.

An important point too, especially in relation to the reluctant believer or seeker after the faith, is Zundel's repeated affirmation, perhaps most apparent in *The Interior Gospel*, that evangelism, the central Christian duty of spreading God's word, is not so much a question of talking about God or Christ. It is rather a question of communicating a quality of inner being or light through one's way of being and of relating to the 'other'. To this extent, evangelism continually puts one's own faith to the test, for it requires one to accede to one's full stature as a human being or 'person' implicit in God's image of one as a personal creation, and to live authentically in the light of that image. His message is as important to the believer as to the one who may still be searching.

The sermons, then, have been chosen with a broad readership in mind, and to give a glimpse of the essential Zundel. Inevitably, amongst readers who may have some prior knowledge of Zundel, there is likely to be some dispute over the word 'essential'. If the texts chosen reach out to a wider reading public, and if they challenge the believer and non-believer alike to look at themselves, society and the Church in a new way, the risk and adventure of writing will have been worthwhile.

Translator's Note

A key problem for any translator is the question of equivalences. This is especially so in the case of Zundel who was steeped in Bergsonism, an intrinsic part of the French philosophical tradition since the beginning of the last century. To an Anglo-Saxon empiricist mind-set, there is no real equivalent to the frequently recurring word 'moi', often rendered in the following chapters by the word 'self' or 'being'. The same is true of the words 'élan' and 'devenir', on occasions retained in their original (as is the word 'moi'), for albeit their cultural origin, they are already a part of our common linguistic currency and way of thinking about life and truth.

It is useful to bear in mind, too, the depth and richness of meaning of the words 'intelligence' and 'sens' in French, likely to be core terms in any work dealing with ultimate ends. 'Sens' in particular, with its triple meaning of sense or sensation, meaning, and purpose or direction, can be a richly suggestive if tantalizing word to translate.

Such examples give just an inkling of the hazards of the translator's art. Yet it is precisely in the difficulties that the allure lies. This, ideally, is the case for the reader too, who, faced with the hybrid language that is any translation, is engaged in a process of 'sense-making'. And just occasionally, via the labyrinth of words and their circuitous trails, the bounds of consciousness may recede, to give a glimpse of the Word enshrined in silence.

No one was more aware of this than Zundel, as the epilogue will show.

1. The Problem of Man

This is the first of a number of sermons in <u>Your Face My Light</u>
*dealing with a similar question: 'Do you believe in man?', 'I
believe in God because I believe in man', 'The religion of
man'. It seems an appropriate starting point for the
exploration of a writer who was so deeply engaged in the
question of the crisis of faith in the Western world.*

*Does God exist? ...a fairly predictable question, it may be
thought, as a lead-in to his subject. What is not so predictable,
however, is the nature of the response and the lyrical fervour
in places of its expression, initially disorientating perhaps for
an English reader accustomed to more restrained norms of
cultural expression. Unpredictable, then... We touch here on
the essential Zundel, so often original, challenging,
provocative, who turns the question on its head, as it were, to
make an apologia not for God but for man, at least for man
as he might be, yet who, in his evolutionary status, seems so
often to have lost track of himself and, he suggests, to be
hardly distinguishable from the 'animal'. What is the clamour
for freedom about if he has not questioned his own self to
know who he really is or what his prime motivations are? As
is so typical of Zundel, the secular and the spiritual are
immediately intertwined.*

*In this disquisition on modern-day man, who through the
advances of science and psychology is better able than any of
his predecessors to know himself and the creative possibilities
of freedom to direct humanity to its highest purpose, the key
Zundelian concepts are already there: prefabricated being,
self-disappropriation, inner encounter, becoming source,
origin and creator, the self and the other, the person and*

Presence, concepts which will be elaborated upon in succeeding chapters.

Zundel is accused by some of repeating himself. Others may be struck rather by a consistent logic which becomes ever more persuasive as his vision deepens. And always there is his originality. What right-thinking Catholic would be so audacious as to make God dependent on man? Yet that, it may be postulated, is the first part of a syllogism intrinsic to his theology, which depends for its completion on the creative effort of the individual intelligence to comprehend 'being' itself...

* * *

If we want to tackle the problem of the existence of God, the first question we must address is the problem of the existence of man.

It has long been the case that God has ceased to exist for vast numbers of our contemporaries. But the drama is accentuated by the fact that man himself is ceasing to exist. We no longer believe in man, assuming we have ever done so, comparing him to a machine or a computer, every part of which can be explained technically, scientifically in terms of the activity of our molecules and the secret of our passions no less than of our thoughts.

This structuralist vision of man according to which man is basically an object, a mechanism, does not really surprise us, for that in a way is what we are, machines, robots, who do not speak or think for ourselves. Our thoughts and words come ready made. We are prisoners of set modes of speech and strongly held beliefs and attitudes, which are the product of self-interest and self-esteem. It is these which make us what we are. Most of the time we do not exist in our own right.

It is extremely rare for the person to show through in us and express itself in its dignity, authenticity and grandeur. For basically we are prefabricated beings. We have been cast up in the world without any reference to our own will, and when

67

we try to get to the core of who we are, that core is already there, and will always be so…

In this lies the most striking and alarming paradox. We allow ourselves to be imprisoned in our prefabrications or determinisms. We are unwilling to let go, every minute of the day submitting to this 'me' or 'self' which has come to us ready-made, in the construction of which we have played no part.

And that is precisely where the problem lies. Where is the human being in all of this? If we are motivated purely by self-interest and the instinct for self-preservation, is there the slightest difference between our situation as humans and that of plants and animals? If we cling to, automatically subscribe to what does not derive from ourselves, allowing our behaviour to be determined solely by our physical and emotional drives, how can we ever emerge as persons? And what, in this world of ours, does the word 'person' mean?

There lies the fundamental question. Either there is no such thing as man, the human being, and never will be, since he is nothing more than a bundle of physico-chemical determinants and other impulses which have complete control over him. And that is it, there is nothing more to say on the subject. All those words like dignity, grandeur, human rights, love, devotion, goodness, godliness mean nothing; they are hot air; they signify no more than the secretion of our molecules.

If, however, one accepts the premise that man might exist, if one believes in the possibility of man, then he has to be created, and this emergence as a person is our responsibility. How do we go about this task of creation? How, from this prefabricated 'me' and 'self' which exists independently of us, can we rise up as creators, the source and origin of ourselves?

There is only one solution if we wish to go beyond our determinisms, which lead nowhere, only one solution if we feel our lives fixed in an unchanging mould, incapable of shedding one skin for another, as it were. There is only one solution if we wish to become human. It is to take hold of everything we are, we possess, the whole 'bundle' of ourselves, if I can use such a term, and throw it overboard.

The dignity of which I have spoken, the hallmark of our humanity, is only attainable through love. And the love in question is only conceivable, practicable in the light of an encounter in our most intimate being with a Presence which was there waiting for us and which awakens our love because it is immediately apprehended by us as Love absolute.

It is in our innermost being, there only, that this articulation from a human experience to a divine experience can take place. It is only through our encounter with this Presence which is Light, Love, Oblation, supreme Liberty, that we can transcend our carnal self and prefabrications.

It is in our innermost being, therefore, that a true encounter with God takes place, a God who is not a figment of our imagination but, if we are alert to his presence, may be lived, experienced, recognised at every moment of the day, a God who, contrary to everything said about him, reveals Himself as the well-spring of our liberty and of our freedom to create ourselves.

Nothing is more disturbing than to see God being constantly disfigured, absurdly presented as a power exterior to the world and remote from men's lives, absorbed in himself and his own glory and well-being, treating the world as a plaything which he abandons to its fate, the meaning of which is all too clear to us. Nothing is more disturbing than this conception which is so off-putting to a great many of our contemporaries, sincere, serious-minded people though they are, but who have given up any idea of searching for God because of this absurd caricature in their minds.

It is thus of crucial importance to come to grips with the fact that the encounter with God is identical with the encounter with ourselves, our true being, which is still a projection of ourselves, that is to say, it is not yet Itself but is capable of becoming so – that essential self or priceless being ('moi-valeur') which for all those around us, once it is truly alive, can be a force for freedom and a revelation of our humanity.

Humanity is at work, it has discovered human rights. But it has to be understood that it is a 'projection' of ourselves, the creation of each and every one of us through the encounter within our own being with Love Infinite, which is always there waiting but never imposes itself on us.

There is here an amazing ambiguity which for most people turns the whole of religion into an obstacle, an insurmountable problem they prefer not to think about, for the very reason that they have never thought about the problem of man. They have never called their own being into question.

Yet that is where the process has to start. Any reform is doomed to failure if it is the outcome of men's adulterated passions rather than of an inner freedom indicating a breaking out of the barriers of selfhood to be born again and purified, and so become a space of universal self-giving.

That, then, is the answer: to call oneself into question, to delve deep down to the core of one's being where one discovers an alternative: either man does not endure beyond himself and life is absurd; or he can be born again, but in relation to an infinite universe and an unbounded Love which will enable us to break free of our limitations and re-create ourselves as a pure impulse of generosity.

To sum up, the fundamental question today is that of the existence of man. On the one hand is the fact of our lack of authenticity, of our tendency to perpetuate a prefabricated past. On the other there is the failure of so many, including the most eminent amongst us, to call their own selves into question. Most people accept themselves as they are, slaves of their determinisms, and shy away from a life established on the most unambiguous and most hard-won truths.

It is only by living authentically and in an attitude of total generosity that we will come face to face in our innermost selves with the Eternal.

('Le problème de l'homme', *Your Face My Light*, pp.15-19, extracts.)

***

Echoes and Reflexions: The Written Word

(i)

Everything said about God in human language comes from man. There is no telephone in heaven transmitting directly to us knowledge about God. All we can know about God – even the most authentically inspired words – necessarily comes to us via a human mind and would be bound by the limits of its own situation, were the mind in question not able to go beyond itself and instil into the words and images which derive from it an emerging and enveloping light, conferring on the words a transcendent meaning through which God becomes an intimate part of ourselves.

One may better understand the scope of these reflexions, if only by way of illustration, through these diary jottings of mine: 'Florence, the Médicis Chapel'. My first encounter with Michael Angelo outside of books. There are just the two of us, myself and a friend. Not a sound. Complete silence. A sense of peacefulness in the space around where every figure seems to breathe. It is not as in most museums where one's eyes ache from too much looking. This repose or relaxation excludes any pretence of enthusiasm. I am not looking for anything in particular. My mind is free, I am simply looking. My eyes range tranquilly backwards and forwards across the serene melancholy of the *Pensieroso* from 'dawn' to 'dusk', from 'day' to 'night'. Time stands still. A growing influx of timelessness, deep, silent, in an expanding present. The figures recede, disappear into an invisible centre of gravitation, and there is only this centre left now in its own space. And I suddenly feel myself in complete thrall to it. Liberated from my own being as I have never been before. With no memory of myself, no effort to return to myself, totally free, in a state of joyful acceptance of this unconditional offering of myself. I have at last discovered the life of life in me, the secret so long buried in the opaque depths of this self which has just come to life in me. I exist, I have broken free, become a pure élan or aspiration towards this other being in whom I find myself. I was outside; now I am inside. Bound since birth to a biology not chosen by me...my true self was elsewhere. Or rather it had not yet come into being. And now it has risen up from this encounter, with no limits set about it, a sort of space of generosity permeated by a circulating presence which is its source and fulfilment.

I now know the full measure of man. He exists only through this interaction in which 'I is another'... He is a creator only when he becomes an unseen force for liberation in others. He achieves his full stature as a human only when he lets through the light of infinity which makes of him a source and an end.

(From *Do you believe in man? (Croyez-vous en l'homme?)*, Paris, Ed.du Cerf, 2008 [originally published in 1955], pp.42-45, extracts.)

It is to be noted that Zundel is already in 1955 using the phrase '*I is another*' which will be adopted as the title of the book he published in 1971. The text cited undoubtedly dates from his stay in Italy in the middle to late twenties.

(ii)

If it is a question of graduating from being *something* to being *someone*, the first point to establish is what is going on inside a man.[32] Will he stop accepting himself as he is, the product of his biology or genes, the reflexion of his moods, the affirmation of his race or class? Will he rise up as a creator, infused with that space which is the revelation to everyone of their freedom? Will he be elevated to his true self and feel the embrace of a living, silent presence which is both there overwhelming him and not there, continually opening

---

[32] The generic term 'l'homme', which in French shares the same etymology as 'humain', is used throughout Zundel's writings. Retention of the term in English, however politically incorrect, obviates the use of the word 'person' which has very specific connotations in Zundel's work and is a key concept of his theology.

out into a new field of discovery? Will he be the unseen force uniting those who continually rub shoulders but never meet, isolated as they are from each other, imprisoned in their own egos by mutual envy and hate? Will he reveal to them the common treasure, there for their safekeeping in their most intimate self? Will he inscribe into history this dimension of generosity, emerging as an offering, a giving, through which existence bursts forth in its freedom and all people are bound to each other in intimacy and matter itself assumes a human face?

Were there to be only one in a thousand, one in a million who attained this plenitude, but encouraged by others through a collective show of friendship and esteem ready to spark off an identical movement in themselves, it would be with this person in mind that the school, the factory, the farm and community should be organised, making each of these settings an *instrument of humanisation...*

Taking the world of work as one example, it is clear that its structures need to be fundamentally changed if the ultimate objective, rather than to produce goods, is to liberate the human being in each worker.

(Ibid., pp.88-89.)

2. Group Religion and Personal Religion

Perhaps Zundel is such a popular theologian today because of the sympathetic attitude he expresses towards non-believers. As he states in <u>The Interior Gospel</u>, *"People may be shocked by my sympathy for unbelievers, which contrasts so forcibly at times with my severity towards believers." The unbeliever for Zundel is not necessarily one who remains defined by his determinisms, his 'prefabrications'. On the contrary, he (or she) may have a rich inner or spiritual life capable of uplifting him and opening him to a space of generosity and love as much as any conventional Christian illumined by church attendance and teaching. Indeed, because he has, as it were, laboured for himself, he may ultimately arrive at a more authentic faith than the former.*

There is much in Zundel's writings to bring reassurance and guidance to those reluctant or hesitating believers who fail to identify with the Church in its present form. One wonders, in fact, whether he was not counting on such a force to transform the Church from without through testimonies via language of inner revelation or light – for what is that light if not the revelation of a 'Presence'? Might they not enrich our conception of God the creator, God the communicator through the person of His son, whose only written legacy, to our chagrin, was a few words inscribed in the dust? Jesus Christ was not a scribe, he was not ordered like some of the prophets of old to write down God's words in 'the book'. But how otherwise could he have been the Logos, the Word made flesh at a specific moment in time? Logos…the divine wisdom, reason, knowing… Has the Church sufficiently pondered on our rationalist heritage, not as the first nail in the coffin of belief, but as the glory it might signify as a stage in humanity's progress towards the 'City', or ultimate unity of mankind in the light of knowledge and truth?

Whilst the first chapter called the individual into question, demanding a radical examination of oneself in order to recognise where one's true humanity lies, the present chapter turns its attention to the Church and – Zundel suggests – to organised religion, which seemingly has ceased to fulfil its role in helping humanity to find itself. The Church, which today draws only a minority of people to it, and sometimes through habit if not superstition, needs radically to re-examine itself in order to recognise where it is failing the individual, susceptible to so many more disorientating and destructive pressures than in the past. Yet is religious emotion, or what Zundel calls 'fervour', any less evident in people than previously? All one can say is that it manifests itself in more diverse, and arguably, more creative ways, since it derives most often from a personal aspiration or effort of will. Can the Church close its eyes to these expressions of 'personal religion' which, if seemingly incompatible with the language and rituals of the Church collective, point to a common repository of humanity of which Christ himself, Zundel argues, was the precursor or first advocate? In the sermon following, 'personal religion' is elevated to the status of a 'sacrament', equal in importance to 'group religion' in the Church collective seeking itself through History.

***

The vast majority of human beings have not chosen their religion; it has been decided for them by their geography, their group, their tribe. But there comes a moment when this situation is no longer tenable; once having attained a certain level of self-awareness, the individual feels the need to choose for himself and to establish an adult relationship with God, based on freedom.

Today, in fact, we have reached this turning point. Humanity is going through the greatest evolutionary crisis in History in this tension between a community or group religion, the religion one has acquired at birth, and a personal religion one decides on for oneself, as satisfying a yearning that springs up from one's most intimate being.

This crisis is especially pronounced in intellectual circles, but really it can be said to affect the whole of society; for if we truly are living in a so-called atheistic world, this is more as a result of people's objection to communal forms of religion than to the more intimate type of mystical fervour through which the individual pursues his own private and personal ideal.

In Catholicism, for example – to focus on the Church we know best – many people adopt an attitude of detachment towards the Church, not so much through hostility as indifference. As has been suggested, they prefer a religion they have worked out for themselves, one which satisfies their personal needs and comes from the best part of themselves and finds its own forms of devotional expression. 'I don't need to go into a church to pray,' people are heard saying; 'it leaves me bored and dissatisfied. I feel myself infinitely closer to God listening to music.'

The reason why it is so difficult to resolve this crisis is that we have inherited from Judaism a marvellous book which people are returning to more and more, even if there is a lot in it we still don't understand: that is the Bible. In the Bible a good many of the texts concern the tribe. They celebrate God's covenant with a people viewed in its entirety as faithful to God, to the extent that if the covenant is broken the tribe will be punished, even exterminated, except for a faithful remnant who will ensure the continuity of God's worship on earth. It is impossible, indeed, to read the Bible – even the greatest books of the prophets like Isaiah and Jeremiah – without being struck by the collective nature of the Judaic religion. It is the group, the people, the tribe who are in a relationship with God, and the individual only does so by virtue of his belonging to the people through membership of a particular group.

It is true that the Jewish tradition is not the last word on the subject, for the Bible of the Old Testament leads us forward to the Living, Eternal Word of Christ. It cannot be denied, even so, that this biblical tradition and the knowledge associated with it have weighed heavily on the history of Christianity.

In the Middle Ages, the Byzantine Church and the Church of the West continued this group tradition. When Charlemagne converted the Saxons, he imposed on them the practice of Lent fasting under penalty of death. The traditional belief still held good that religion was a group concern, a national concern, and could be imposed by the sword because it was one of the institutions necessary to the survival of a secure, well-regulated state.

If we take the example of Switzerland and the case of two men from adjoining regions, the one Catholic because he was born in the Valais, the other Protestant because he was born in the Vaud, we see that the tradition has been maintained right down to the present day. In matters pertaining to the political and religious configuration of the country, history has a much greater say than personal choice.

So we arrive at the situation today where there is a sort of conflict – that, at least, is how it feels – between the aspirations of the individual and the demands of the community. The Church has become a tiresome duty to which people grudgingly conform; it is no longer the spring of fresh, living water of which Jesus spoke to the Samaritan woman at Jacob's well. That is why so many people are expressing their religious fervour outside the official boundaries of the Church.

There are some amazing scientists like Pierre and Marie Curie, Einstein, and Jean Rostand, who dedicate to their pursuit of truth not only their scientific genius but all they possess of generosity and love. There are artists and writers like Flaubert and Nietzsche who have accorded the greatest importance to the perfecting of rhythm, harmony, and expression, because through language they felt themselves in communion with Eternal Beauty. This is true, too, of many musicians like Beethoven, Bach and Mozart, who in their case were Christians.

It is clear, however, that a great many people who listen to their music are not Christians; and yet they are just as receptive to the spiritual truth the music transmits. Then there are those who experience through the *ballets russes* something they are unable to experience in a church. It is their way of finding God, of paying homage to a Presence within, of going beyond their own being and becoming a space of generosity.

What is our position in relation to this question? One thing is certain: we cannot close our eyes to the problem. We must seek a balance between a personal religion which satisfies our tastes, our highest and worthiest aspirations, our enthusiasms, our commitment to the present, and a group religion.

Many Catholics do not have a personal religion. They come to church and respect collective observances and rituals such as praying aloud, but they have no conception whatsoever of their relationship with God as signifying a marriage of love in which God's Face is imprinted in their hearts, or as a personal encounter which is inexhaustible in the light and joy it brings. They simply identify with the group and do not think beyond it, good and honest worshippers though they are, and that already means a great deal. But they have never known the tremor of joy of the mystic which has produced great poems like the *Canticle to the Sun* of St Francis of Assisi or *The Spiritual Canticle* of St John of the Cross. Perhaps they are content with things as they are. Fortunately, however, there are a great many people who are not.

Those who do not experience a true love or passion for God, sealed by a nuptial relationship with Him such as is evoked by St Paul in the Second Letter to the Corinthians ('I have espoused you to one husband, that I may present you as a chaste virgin to Christ' [II Co, 11:2]), will be carried away by other enthusiasms or passions. And it is precisely those

78

with the richest personalities, those who are the most gifted, creative and dynamic, who are caught up in the maelstrom because they have only known a community or group God, a God exterior to themselves. They have never contracted that personal relationship with God which is an unending process of discovery and enrichment.

What is Christ's attitude to this question? It is clearly Christ Himself who has inclined our thoughts in the direction outlined. For it is immediately apparent that he was Himself a victim of community religion. He was sacrificed in the name of the group, condemned to death as an enemy of it. As the high priest Caiaphas affirmed: 'It is expedient for us that one man should die for the people that the whole nation perish not' (Jn11:50).

Jesus, in fact, was an endless source of anxiety to the Judaic community, which was so perfectly organised at the time. They felt He was evading their rules, undermining their traditions and was a threat to the unity of the nation.

So it is clear that Christ is not going to discourage us from having a personal religion. The contrary is the case; He will expect it of His followers. But at the same time – and here lies the paradox – they will be required to have a community religion too.

For Christ – and Paul expresses it magnificently in his Letters from Captivity – is the One who brings down the barriers between people and seeks to unite everyone in His own Person. His religion, therefore, will necessarily have a universal character. He will deliberately choose to create a chain of love in which all peoples, all individuals, every soul, every single person will be linked together as one.

How, then, can we reconcile this community requirement, so perfectly expressed in the term 'catholic', which means universal, with the persistent, deep-seated desire in us for a personal religion?

It is by means of the Sacrament. And by this I mean not only the seven sacraments which go by this name, but the Church in all its manifestations: people, books, doctrines, rituals, material artefacts.

But what exactly is a sacrament? Put briefly, and to give a concrete illustration, it is akin to a gesture of tenderness, the 'Yes' one utters to the partner in marriage, the kiss the mother bestows on her sleeping child – gestures which are clearly visible but only mean something because they come from within.

There is, therefore, a system of signs or symbols regulating all human relationships, but they only mean something if they come from inside the person. So if there is no-one behind the sign, it becomes meaningless.

'The whole of the outside must be embraced by the inside': that is the fundamental principle underlying any sacramental institution. So when we state that the Church is the mystical body of Christ, we are saying just that: the Church is a symbol which can be comprehended only from within, through a rigorous effort of mystical understanding. One has to be in a state of mystical union with Christ to comprehend the riches, the grandeur and the beauty of the Church's mystery, which exists under the veil of signs.

Unless we come face to face with Christ, we will continue to feel crushed by the group or community religion imposed on us by our geography or heredity.

The whole crisis of the Reformation would have turned out differently, had it been understood that a Catholic or Christian cannot be a living member of the Church without a personal religion, for the Christian community is grounded in the solitude of Faith, Hope and Love.

But it must be clear to anyone meditating on these words in the silence of their own inner self that they take on a specific colouring according to the person one is. It is like being at a concert and feeling oneself carried away with everyone else by the music and experiencing a marvellous sense of human unity. Yet one experiences this unity in the solitude of one's own heart.

It is at the moment of total solitude, when we are lost in the deepest recesses of our own being, that we experience a sense of true communion with others, in so far as they have attained the same state of solitude themselves. There is a sort of pulsation of life shared by all in the face of a Presence which belongs to all, yet it remains the most personal secret of each one in the intimacy of their own being.

('Religion de groupe et religion personnelle', *Your Face My Light*, pp.79-85, extracts.)

***

Echoes and Reflexions: The Written Word

Religion is not attached exclusively to any particular organisation or set of procedures. Religion is life itself, in its plenitude, open to the divine Presence and transfigured by it.

It follows that outside of the communal liturgy which assembles people on a Sunday round the Lord's Table, everyone whilst carrying out their daily work or routine can find something to pray about.

No specific formula is necessary, no specific words, no specific request. All that is required is a willingness of mind and readiness to accept everything God is and wants to be in us, beyond anything that we ourselves can comprehend.

Some people find their nourishment in the Bible or the lives of the saints, others in the varied spectacles of nature or in scientific research, others in artistic endeavour or in the pleasure of teaching, in looking after the sick, or in marvelling at the innocence of children.

This is not to say that all these experiences are equal in value. It is simply acknowledging how beneficial it is, whilst still according the first importance to liturgical prayers in church, to seek out in our daily lives situations which automatically give rise to the desire to pray and to sustain our souls in a state of unity with God.

Many people have lost interest in those prayers consisting of two or three set formulae; these have long since lost all meaning and substance for them. But there are as many ways of praying as there are encounters in a day. And listening in silence is the finest one of all.

All those artists who have produced something truly great acknowledge that they reached the high point of their art when it was no longer themselves creating. They were simply following the dictates of a mysterious Source with which they felt themselves one.

The human person is a seat of initiative. As a 'person' we aspire to be a source, as we are destined to be an end. Something in the universe must come into being through us, which could not be there without us. We are not truly human unless we radiate through life greater truth and love.

It seems that humanity has rarely expressed with such violence its spiritual vocation; it has rarely expressed such a grievous, heart-felt longing for the divine city, in which everyone, through a truly personal activity and unceasing creative life, could express all the energies of their soul, their inner life – that divine city which haunted the prophets' dream as a vision of peace, and which in reality is the Church envisioned by Christ.

What a sacrament each person would be for us if we sought out in them the divine idea which is their true *identity*, if we approached them with the desire to uncover that part of the Infinite in them which is there to radiate through them.

Christian detachment is precisely this divine passion for people's grandeur and the refusal to recognise anything less in them than the nobility of their origin and their end; it is our desire to see them *be*.

Sin is the refusal of this plenitude, the arbitrary limitation of oneself, renunciation of the spirit, yielding to matter, slipping into the abyss of night.

Often we are taken in by success, dazzled by decorations, flattered by titles, subjugated by wealth. We love the sound of our own voice, chase after the right people, those who can help us to get on.

But all of that belongs to a world outside of us. Our soul recognises the emptiness of it all once we recollect our true nature. And this is most likely to happen when we experience through someone we meet a genuine expression of goodness.

We were there just as on other days, doing the same things, expressing the same attitudes, and this light suddenly flows past us, revealing beyond the stultifying routine of our days the sense of a Presence, still obscure but recognisable in the emotion we feel. It is like dawn lighting up a cathedral nave, gradually illuminating the dull glass of the windows with a diaphanous light which reveals a heavenly choir singing the Canticle to the Sun.

Anyone who has had this experience knows it has nothing to do with race, culture, origins, age or sex.

Every human being is capable of bestowing this marvellous gift which reveals to the other the true nature of our humanity. And those who have done so remain forever our benefactors, even if we have met them only once, in a passing encounter... They are a true revelation to us: the revelation of the light of life revealed in the transparency of a being through whom shines the divine Face.

(From *The Interior Gospel*, op.cit., pp.77-80, 100, 123, 135, 137-9.)

3. Beauty or the Encounter with God: An Amazing Adventure

Why is it that church worship so often leaves us bored or unenthusiastic and we treat it as a ritual carried out more as an obligation than from a true desire to enter into God's presence and renew our spirit, with all that signifies of furthering love and human understanding? Yet we are drawn spontaneously to other spheres of activity, such as the enjoyment of nature, which testify to the religious spirit in us and its craving for nourishment.

Zundel focuses in this sermon on the idea of Beauty as a manifestation of the divine and as a liberation of the human spirit, an experience which was crucial to the faith of the great saints and mystics who saw language as a key component of that beauty. Music is often cited as the most spiritual of the arts, yet the first sentence in the prologue to St John underlines the priority of the Word, the Word mysteriously made flesh. The concept is reversed in Zundel's theology to become 'the flesh made Word', a metaphor for the idea of language as the spiritual prerogative of man as he grapples with the expression of Beauty and Truth.

Beauty, which elevates man to his true status, is revealed in so many aspects of human life. But none of them, Zundel argues, matches up to the Beauty one feels in the encounter with God, which he illustrates by reference to St Augustine's moment of conversion, his transcending experience of a 'Beauty always ancient and always new'. Such a moment will be the start of a most amazing adventure of rebirth, grounded in a sustained inner searching which opens one more and more to the sense of one's infinity and the infinity of others, and testifies to the transcending presence through man of God in History. What a vocation and what a destiny!

The question remains, in relation to the call to man to perpetuate God's act as 'origin, source, and creator' of himself and to be a living light in the world to others, of the Church's role as mediator between the divine and the human, the earthly and the eternal, and of its adaptation to the changing condition of modern man, subject to ever-increasing material pressures yet still drawn to a truth beyond the material.

* * *

I had the occasion recently to re-read *The Spiritual Canticle* of St John of the Cross, and I was particularly struck by this verse: "Let us rejoice, Beloved, let us see ourselves in Your Beauty." His commentary on these words is astonishing in its outpouring of lyricism. In the space of a few lines the word 'Beauty' recurs a score of times: "Let us see ourselves in your Beauty: I will see myself in Your Beauty, I will be me in Your Beauty and You will be me in Your Beauty…"

It is impossible to utter these words without realizing that for St John of the Cross, as for all mystics, contact with God is what generates life and enthusiasm; for it is a nuptial bond, one in which the person is exchanged in the deepest, the most intimate part of itself with God; the person, indeed, comes into being through this giving or offering of itself, and from this point on is in a perpetual state of wonder at its own sense of growing and coming closer to perfection.

Between the pages of this mystic, so full of poetry and grandeur, and the religion of our parishes…well, what do they have in common? In our parishes people often seem so dull and apathetic, as though religious life is a chore, a duty, something one has to do because one is in the hands of a being who will one day exercise power of judgment over one, and it is safer, after all, to put the odds on one's side.

Yes, people are bored in our churches. I am frequently bored myself because everything seems so dull and grey and predictable; week in week out one goes on churning out the same old words... But for the mystic God is a fire burning deep in his heart, as He was for Pascal on the famous night of his conversion.

It is surprising what strategies one sometimes has to resort to when administering the sacraments, precisely because the Christian life – or what we call by that name – has become a set of rituals to which people automatically conform, even if, admittedly, with the best of intentions. It is anything but a discovery of joy, exhilaration, a renewal of fervour before the revelation of God's Beauty. Least of all is it an amazing adventure which gives a permanent savour to life as we awaken each day to a new world.

Look at the adventure of science. If you open a science book or a good science magazine, every page will fill you with wonder as you come face to face with a new discovery or a new dimension of the universe. You are bowled over by these testimonies to human intelligence which has established man's rule over matter; and from the earth, man can now look to the stars and the possibility of exploiting forms of energy once inconceivable to him.

Art too is an adventure. On certain days one would see Clara Haskil leave the concert platform with a drawn look on her face, because she felt her performance had fallen short of the mark. For one never knows if one is going to be up to the occasion, capable of expressing Beauty, of transferring to one's fingers the melody which flows through one's heart. One never knows if the public has truly responded to the creative spirit behind the work, that eternal, self-renewing source from which all human masterpieces through History have derived.

Mountaineering too is an adventure and men of the most remarkable courage are drawn to it by the danger it represents. They put their own lives at risk because of this fascination and their desire to live life to the full. By risking death and emerging unscathed, life becomes all the more enjoyable and exhilarating.

And those not capable of scientific or artistic achievements or facing life-threatening challenges, go to football matches and stand there freezing for hours as they watch the ball being kicked to and fro over a frozen pitch. This activity too has its value, for it is a way of appreciating the skill and agility and elegance and muscular strength and all the other expressive dimensions of the human body.

And what do we Christians do whilst the crowds go and freeze for hours at a sporting event? So often, outside the customary hours of Sunday mass, our churches are virtually empty, because people are bored there; they don't see the Christian life as an adventure; they don't realise that whatever man's scientific, artistic and sporting achievements, there is a need, a value in him infinitely greater than the forms of creativity just mentioned, however admirable in themselves. It is the adventure leading to self-creation, in which man's entire being is transformed into a source, an origin, a boundless space; and through this adventure man will leave his mark on History and change its course, raising up Humanity in a divine gesture of eternal, self-giving Love.

Are we blind? Yes we are, for we do not see the Cross shining out on the tops of our churches, holding out its arms to us as our one true hope in life. Cannot we see the Cross as a measure of the infinity and grandeur of our lives? For that is what the Cross signifies: that God died to ensure our victory as humans. Yes, there is something so amazing in us that nothing less than God's death was required to ensure its realisation.

So, then, it is not a question of running away from life, of turning our backs on existence, of asking ourselves questions about an after-life. Heaven is here, now, within us! Yes, there is an infinitely more exciting adventure to be lived than climbing a mountain, or mastering the universe, or satisfying an artistic impulse. We ourselves are at its core, called to become so precious, so great, so lovely that Heaven indeed appears to be within us and to shine through us. Our face transmits a sense of the divine, eternal Presence.

That, then, is the adventure we are called to engage in, nothing less: to reveal God's presence, to show Him alive in History, and to demonstrate his Light and Love in all the actions of our life. The Christian life is a huge adventure, since it puts God's very existence at stake; for God has no other way of entering History, except through us.

('La Rencontre de Dieu: l'aventure la plus passionnante', *Your Face My Light*, pp.103-106, extracts.)

***

Echoes and Reflexions: The Written Word

(i)

Hymn to Beauty and the Adventure of Being

If, like St Augustine, one considers that the knowledge of man and the knowledge of God are interdependent, one immediately realises that man himself is called into question every time he asks a question about God.

One learns from the *Confessions* that one cannot come to know God without first coming to know oneself, and that the true encounter with God comes from within... A new world comes into being in which contact with others results from an impulse of generosity which is an act of total, unconstrained self-giving and an expression of love.

In this connection there is nothing more spontaneous, less artificial, constructed than this confidence which follows on from his hymn to Beauty, so often quoted: "You called me, you cried out to me, and you broke through my deafness; you shone, resplendent, and put my blindness to flight; You exhaled your perfume and I breathed it in. I came breathlessly towards You, I tasted You and was hungry and thirsty; You touched me and set me on fire and I was drawn into Your peace."[33]

The words are bursting to express the ineffable, but their very cadences make us feel the breathless wonderment Augustine himself felt as he suddenly discovered God to be the Life of his life.

That, indeed, is what is communicated to us two lines later: 'I will be truly Living when my life is filled by You'. The moment of conversion is clearly only the first step of an itinerary he will pursue to the very end: 'Now, since You are raising up the one whom You are permeating with your Presence, since you have not yet taken complete possession of me I must continue my search for you.'

('Quel Dieu ? in *Hymn to Joy [Hymne à la joie]*, Ed. Anne Sigier, 1992, pp.43-45, extracts.)

(ii)

Nature

Whoever has felt a sense of wonder contemplating a landscape and feeling it penetrate to the depths of his being, confirming his sense of unity and harmony with the universe, has to admit that Nature, to which we are bound in a physical relationship which is cruelly restrictive, nevertheless sometimes conspires to free us from this bond and go beyond it in an act of self-transcendence... Our symbiosis with the physical world comprises not only a side of our nature turned towards our relation to the animal world, but also a side turned towards an exit point where we are released from our earth-bound nature, through an Encounter which opens us, now weightless, to a limitless, transcendent space within us.

Since time immemorial artists have experienced this spiritual communion with the material and expressed it magnificently in words, for example Gorki, and Keats, in

---

[33] *Confessions*, Book X, pp.27-28, Penguin.

these lines which enshrine an amazing density, simplicity, and incantatory power:

And then there crept

A little noiseless noise among the leaves

Born of the very sigh that silence heaves.

Could any words evoke more effectively the unspoken polyphony of silence, like a presence murmuring within us?

Thus Nature can reveal itself as the abode of silence from which all great works of art derive: but first among these is man, who can only become a creator by listening to the original Music which, on his deathbed, Bach said no man would ever succeed in writing.

('La nature', Ibid., pp.21-24, extracts.)

(iii)

Beauty, the Church and Human Diversity

God's most moving gift to us is to have adorned with beauty the world we live in, and by teaching us to discover within every human being the treasure of an infinite love.

Grace does not destroy nature; it adds a new dimension to it, just as the artist, in the frame of his canvas, creates an illusion of boundless space.

And what is true of the elements which have become the substance of the sacraments is even more true of humans who must find their being through this same matter. Christianity's dream is not to cut men off from their earthly roots by imposing on them a faceless uniformity, which would make them unreal, no more than it is the artist's desire always to sketch the same portrait on the basis that Beauty is one, indivisible, and that is the truth he has to express. The very opposite is the case: it is through the singularities of his subject that he must tease out their mystery, and his work will come closer to perfection the more he throws into relief the characteristic traits of the face he is trying to capture against an interior light attesting to an infinite Presence.

The universality of the Gospels is not a question of spreading throughout the world a particular human culture with its own mode of expression or sensibility and imposing it on others to whom it may seem alien; it is a question of attributing to human diversity, which is a product of soil, climate and tradition, a universal value by allowing each individual to develop the gift of their singularity, so that every part of them is consecrated to the order of love. Each person needs to hear himself addressed by his name, to feel that all his energies are engaged in the life he embraces, and to realise that the Church is truly his home, a place of intimacy and belonging where he receives love and understanding.

Some will undoubtedly argue that uniformity is the surest way to guarantee unity. One might as well argue that a symphony, to express perfect harmony, can make do with a single instrument. What makes the beauty of the universe is precisely its endless variety, which with each step we take in life offers us the joy of new encounters and makes life itself an endless process of discovery. The Church's truly catholic vocation is proclaimed in its power to magnify the uniqueness of every individual human being.

('The byzantine expression of the Catholic Church', in *The World's Beauty in our Hands, [La beauté du monde entre nos mains]*, Ed. Anne Sigier, 2004, pp.109-111, extracts.)

4. All True Music Is Sacred

This homily may seem to be very much a recapitulation of the previous one with its focus on the arts as a principal means of engaging with the divine within us and of reaching through to the divine in others. Whilst Zundel discourses at one time or another on all of the arts, it is music which has the priority. His work is so imbued with music that no introduction to him would be complete without a text on music specifically, especially one which, as here, so profoundly affects his use of language itself. For language, clearly, was Zundel's own expressive medium, yet one which in practice, his many reflections on the subject suggest, he felt himself to fall far short of deploying creatively, that is, in a spiritually satisfying way.

This text – amongst others in a similar vein scattered through his work – surely conveys a different view. For once he has established his subject and passes from the conceptual to his own subjective engagement with the ideas, he is carried away by lyricism, by the pulsating rhythms of the heart rather than the dictates and sequences of the mind. Phrases, sentences, synonyms, images accumulate, flow into each other in a chant-like stream of sound, interspersed with sighs or exhalations which act as the silences of musical expression he is seeking to analyse, signifying a new breath, a new articulation, a deepening perception. Zundel's language becomes music, recapitulation, harmony, abstraction. His words seem ultimately to be stripped of their substance to achieve pure 'transparency', an aura of light which is ultimately its own object, supplanting everything which has gone before.

Zundel's language, it is true, is often beyond us, discourages us by its profundity, its symbolism, its abstraction, its other-worldliness. How can we ever feel like he did, respond like he did, know like he did? He was, after all, a mystic who lived on the sublimest heights where words, ideas, feelings interfuse to form a language beyond the usages of normal life. Yet there are the periods between – perhaps approximating to the tuneless intrusions and play of discordant instruments in a musical arrangement – when he addresses us in a common everyday language and adduces examples which bring us back to the known world – an old peasant woman, a retarded child, and – yes – Zundel himself. For suddenly he plunges back into our world, is one with us, confronted by the trials and tribulations and frustrations of earthly being. How often, in accordance with the general nature of his subject, does he not start his meditation, as here, in the third person, to switch mid-paragraph to the first person 'we' or 'I' and total identification with those he is addressing, or 'serving'? For every act of Zundel's is a washing of the disciples' feet, an act of humility, of making the other greater than oneself.

And through him music is there, everywhere, accessible to everyone, from the greatest to the least, whether it be in the rustling of a leaf or the pulsating finale of a symphony suddenly fading into silence. We have all, to a greater or lesser degree, experienced the power of music, known its fleeting illuminations, the glimpses it gives of a different reality and a different 'I'. Yet so often we hardly give it time to register and we allow life, reality to come rushing back in.

Zundel, in this homily, goes beyond the previous one, summoning us now to an act of engagement. It is precisely not to let the moment pass, not to let silence be ousted, obliterated by our noisy, physiological surface being. It is to hold on to it, to delve deeper, to silently contemplate the mysterious transformation in us and seek to become its permanent expression. It is to be a living music whose sounds reverberate outwards to others, like the light of the painter's model: a

*simple peasant woman mysteriously pointing to her forehead,
or a retarded child smiling joyously up into its mother's face.*

***

Music, as its name indicates, is the service of the Muses.

Music is, then, a service of the divine. Dinu Lipatti expressed this as well as anyone when, listening to a Beethoven quartet on the day of his death, he declared: "To write beautiful music, you have to be God's instrument." Music, then, participates in the sacred and is situated in a domain of sanctity, so it must find its rightful place.

What exactly is the sacred and how does it get a hold over us?

A peasant woman living in the 17th century pointed to her forehead and said, "Right there, one particular day..." One particular day! That simple exclamation is remarkable! She felt herself in the presence of an all-enveloping light, and that day...well, it sums up the mystery of the human person.

Where is man? How do we recognise him? How do we define him? Where is he to be found? Is it not in that secret place where our life is rooted in God?

There is a perfect identity between them, for to encounter man and to encounter God is one and the same thing. Beyond our emotional life and through it, beyond our intellect and deeper than any part of us, there is light, infinite, eternal day, and that precisely is the person.

The person, what an amazingly appropriate word! ...the person (per-son), the being through whom ('per') music resonates ('sonne'), eternal, infinite music, living music, the music which is God.[34]

---

[34] There is a rich play of words here in the terms 'personne' and 'résonne' in the original French text. Elsewhere in his writings he takes the word 'personne' back to its syntactic roots as consisting of two elements, per-sonne: 'per' (cf. 'par'), 'through' and 'sonne': sounds, resonates. The person thus signifies for Zundel the idea of interior, interpersonal communication.

A mentally handicapped or retarded child, any person, in fact, deprived of the normal use of reason still carries within them this source of light, which is situated at a deeper level than the intellect for it is the light of the heart…the light which is the revelation of an infinite Presence.

That is what we mean by the Sacred: that deepest, most authentic, most infinite, most eternal part of ourselves…which is yet more than ourselves, a limitless, unbounded space of light and love open to everything. It is that part of us which can become for others a wellspring of joy and liberty.

That is where we are to be found, that is our place of being. When we truly exist, that is where our treasure and riches lie. Is it not true, in fact, that we have just seen an entire people demonstrating its desire for freedom,[35] which means exactly that: acceding to this inner space in us and the power to become an origin, a creator, a source, a universe.

And these are not just empty words. This is where the whole of human reality lies: in these depths which can only be reached by love, stirred into being by goodness, find their harmonisation through art.

So what is music about? What is its purpose other than to find the rhythm expressing the unity of the movement? What does music seek to do other than to bring order into our inner being…regulating our heart-beats, the pulsation of our blood, the tempo of our breathing and of our nerve reflexes…so that we ourselves can become harmony, acquire unity and enter into that state of silence where we begin to listen?

Yes, that is the miracle of music: it is to reach into man's innermost depths, but without violating his own inner sanctuary; it is to bring him face to face with the eternal within him, to make visible the Face which is always there ready to engage him in a dialogue with Someone, a dialogue which rescues us from our solitude and liberates our highest powers of intelligence and love, in an act of surrender of ourselves

---

[35] Zundel is referring here to the situation in Hungary in 1956.

which is the ultimate expression of our being, the divine operation of mind, heart and spirit.

But if this dialogue really takes place, if music does give rise to this silent exchange in us through which we encounter the infinite Presence and a movement of divine generosity which generates the same in ourselves and that limitless space where our freedom can truly breathe, it puts us at the same time under an obligation.

If there truly is Someone and we are not alone, if at the source of all music there is this eternal, living music which only silence is attuned to, but which we destroy by the noise and disruption of our lives when our physiological rhythms are no longer in harmony with it, then this dialogue becomes an act of engagement. We have to protect this music, we have to take it into ourselves as a treasure of infinite value; we have to breathe in harmony with it, become its living expression. Our entire being must become 'music'.

This is true of art in general. No artistic masterpiece comes into being outside of silence. At the moment of creativity the artist is always a person listening, a person who surrenders his own being and becomes transparent to the infinite Presence, able to inscribe into the work this infinite dimension, which transcends the limits of matter and through matter enables us to triumph over matter. 'To triumph over': the term is not quite adequate to the idea! Rather is it a question of glorifying matter, of inscribing in it the Face of the Divine.

That is why the vocation of artist is a vocation of saintliness, if saintliness implies precisely this: being permeable to the light, being always attuned to the rhythm of eternity, being this living melody which echoes the divine music.

The artist creates only in a state of total dispossession of himself, and we truly hear or see his work and are nourished by it only when we return to the Source and become silence ourselves, in a supreme act of contemplation engaging our whole being.

"Art is contemplation," said Rodin. It is in the mystery and atmosphere which envelop the finest works that our spirit divines the spirit animating nature and our own self; for all art proceeds from a centre of germination and unfolds from the inside to the outside. It is thus clear that if we focused our lives on art – the artist as well as ourselves, that is – we would permanently be a part of that harmonious, creative rhythm and our own being would be transformed into divine music.

Mozart intuitively knew this from the threshold of eternity where his life hovered, poverty stricken that he was, reliant on others, condemned to such a premature death... Mozart, whose voice broke as he listened to the 'Lacrymosa' of his *Requiem* which – he now recognised – he had written for himself.

The whole of his rich, short life which is still there with us, a source of enduring enchantment, elevating and transfiguring our own lives, was dominated by this inner music and by dialogue with a Presence which transforms the human into the divine.

So, if man is truly human, it is because he carries within him this light, this divine power, this self-giving love, this joy in music. It is music which has this special power to liberate generous, self-giving love, by inducing in him a state of listening silence.

How wonderful it would be if everyone could listen to music and open themselves to its message, to true music, that is, which comes out of contemplation, the music of silence. It would change everything. There would be no more fallings-out, no more separations, for everyone would have returned to the Source, which opens us to our common humanity and to responsibility for the treasure entrusted to us: the Life of God within us, which is the common property of all, yet the most secret possession of each one of us.

It is true, then, that music is the service of the Muses! It is a service of the divine. All true music is sacred because its purpose is to order and harmonise the physiological rhythms of our being and every part of ourselves and transform them into a living music. Its purpose above all is to enable us to encounter the true face of man, in which is reflected the Face of the infinite, a Face which, as its full transparency shines through, reveals the Face of God Himself.

('Toute vraie musique est sacrée', *Your Face My Light*, pp.440-444, extracts.)

***

Echoes and Reflexions: The Written Word

(i)

Art

Is it not true that silence is at one and the same time the basic criterion of the work of art and the effect it seeks to obtain, whatever the medium in question?

That surely accounts for the similar state of being created in us by the most disparate works and forms of expression: the fact that they put us into tune with silence, suppressing the inner noise and turmoil our possessive self continually subjects us to.

If this cathartic effect is not felt and we are not 'cured of ourselves' by a sort of 'conversion to the human', it is because we have not really got inside the work, or because it is not a true work of art.

But if the work is truly 'musical' (in the sense of relating to the muses) and the mediator of a divine presence, there is the immediate implication that the author of the work has experienced a 'musical' moment that it is his purpose to share with us.

This is not to say that the work of art does not have other legitimate ends; it is simply saying that art, to be art, is orchestrated around the concert of relationships between the material elements of the work and is rigorously focused on the effect this process of ordering and harmonisation is capable of producing.

If one stands by the true requisites of art and accepts that it cannot serve any purpose of propaganda or be complicit with any form of sensuality, but remains, in accordance with its true essence, the language of the ineffable...it will be generally agreed that art offers the highest educative opportunities and should be seen and encouraged as the principal instrument of peace and communion between people.

('L'Art' in *Hymn to Joy*, op.cit., pp.96-101, extracts.)

(ii)

Music, Language and the Liturgy

The vocation of language is to translate discursive thought, but it is also to convey and suggest by inductive means what cannot be said: the Ineffable, which is the true reality. A conversation can leave us discouraged or comforted; it can arouse in us, however vaguely, an impression of pleasure or discomfort. A word overheard can fill us with darkness or, on the contrary, with permanent light. Often, though, it is what is not said rather than what is said that matters most, the atmosphere the words convey, the darkness or light one lets into them.

That is why language is so close to music, the language of the ineffable. It is why speech so readily turns into chant: so that the word is not detached from the current from which it issues and can well up in all its dynamic power and potential to move people.

Music, then, uses and amplifies in its own way the living flow of the language, restoring to it the vivifying rhythms and vibrations lost to ideas in its will to abstraction.

One can appreciate, therefore, why the Christian liturgy has been unable to develop without music, and especially the help of chant, since its fundamental aim is to put us into contact with the living, eternal Word...which was made flesh and came to dwell amongst us. Doesn't the underlying mystery of every word lie beyond what it may signify in human terms? Does it not lie in the connection with this Living Word, which is a person, and in retaining a trace of it?

It is natural, therefore, that the sacred texts have taken on the character of chant, their music seeking to translate the divine aura enveloping the words. Psalmody is indisputably the highest expression of this aspiration.

One knows full well one will never express God and that the important thing is to let God speak for Himself in the abysses of silence where his Word comes into being.

That is why psalmody is an art of listening rather than of singing. In its highest expression it is a spiritual, interior music, both human and divine, contemplative and mystical.

(*Poem of the Holy Liturgy [Le Poème de la Sainte Liturgie]*, Paris, *Desclée*, 1998, pp.77-80, extracts.)

5. The Interior God

At the risk of repeating ideas already introduced in passing in the previous chapters, this chapter homes in on the central theme of Zundel's theology which was there almost from the beginning and is reflected in the title of one of his earliest works, The Interior Gospel. It homes in at the same time – for the one is inseparable from the other – on the core premises of St Augustine's Confessions at the root of the latter's conversion, which were a major formative influence on the development of Zundel's theology.

The lyrical, irrepressible flow of Zundel's language, such a challenge to the translator writing for a different 'culture' (as signifying a mode of thinking, feeling, and expressing the world) resonates particularly with those key citations recounting Augustine's conversion, which recur so frequently throughout Zundel's writings. Repetitions they are, but can we see them as anything less, symbolically, than the rock, petrus, on which his personal religion, like the Church, was founded? For yes, to refer back to the title of Chapter 2, Zundel's religion – or in his case 'theology' – was a highly personal and original one, yet one feels the more one reads him, an irrefutable one, so concordant is it with Christ's teaching and the inner language of the Gospels, particularly John.

Poetic language – Zundel decried the word 'discourse' which for him designated the language of the 'outer person' – frequently has recourse to metaphor. Zundel's is no exception. Whilst the term 'nuptial bond', a frequently recurring one in his writings and evocative of the primacy of the Biblical concept, does not occur precisely as such, the great climax of the homily is the idea of 'sealing the gold ring of our eternal engagement'.

The lyricism and poetic fancy of so much of this homily should not cloud one to a core rationalist concept present throughout, and which has such a potential force in today's world: the inviolable freedom of the human being to give meaning and shape to his destiny through acknowledgment of the divine mystery and eschewing the entrapments of 'social' being.

***

Great writers are those who can make words vibrate with an eternal light by the way they put them together, arrange them, balance them one against the other: 'Man is only a reed, the most fragile in nature, but he is a thinking reed'. This immortal saying of Pascal, with its contrast between the fragile and thinking reed transformed into the arbiter of the world, is one of these great sayings which will be with us for all times.

St Augustine is another of these great artists, especially when he is least consciously seeking to achieve an effect and allows himself to be carried away by the spontaneity of his genius and religious fervour to create perfectly crafted words or utterances, which take us into the radiant depths of his inner being.

This is especially so in the *Confessions* where he recounts in the utmost detail his profligate, unruly life followed by his conversion and baptism, praising God unceasingly for having called him to the Light. He expresses his state of being before the conversion in words so admirably simple they convey a direct sense of the eternal light. He says: "Too late was I in loving you, beauty at once so ancient and so new, too late; and yet you were there inside me; but I was outside." (X: 27).

What a wonderful way of putting it: "You were there inside me, but I was outside." That is the situation of the person who has not yet encountered God – to be outside of himself, a phrase reminiscent of the one we use to describe someone who is 'beside himself', as when we say someone is beside himself with anger.[36] He is no longer in control of himself, master of his actions, his conduct; he is outside…a stranger to himself. Man's real condition, however, is to be 'inside', a radiating source for all that is pleasing, harmonious, luminous and creative in his life.

Pursuing his reflections, Augustine adds no less effectively: "You were with me but I was not with you." So God was already there in him, from the beginning, like a hidden sun waiting to break through; it was he himself who was not with God.

We see straightaway, then, that the God he encountered was a God interior to himself, just as he is interior to us, a God who is inside whilst we are outside. And we can deduce that Augustine did not meet God until he went inside himself.

God would call him inside. He would call him to focus his thoughts inwardly, to find his centre, to become a source, an originator of his own conduct, a creator of his life and universe. That is as clear as the words which radiate from the text, for God is inside and we are outside and this intolerable situation, which defines the state of being of the sinner – the situation Augustine was in – can only be overcome when the sinner, a stranger to himself and to God and to the whole world, returns to the inside and establishes that intimate relationship where he can speak to God as Person to Person.

This is an amazing development, for we see through Augustine's journey to God that God's attraction over us is anything but a commandment intended to assert his will, his authority over us. It is the attraction of beauty and a love which seeks to transform us into God's own nature or Being. It seeks to rescue us from our self-dispersal, our weakness, our enslavement, our dependency and draw us to the very heart of our liberty. Once we have found the centre, the intimacy of our own inner being and become a beginning, an origin and a creative source, we shall be face to face with God,

---

[36] The play of words here is not easily translated into English. In French there is a clear syntactic link between 'dehors' (outside) and 'hors de' (beside [in this case 'oneself']).

not as slaves but as friends, interrelating with each other in mutual self-giving love.

This is the God who called Augustine, fascinated his genius, made him into the great Doctor of Grace he was: the Christian God who revealed Himself through Jesus Christ. He is the great liberator who rescues us from our exteriority and transforms us from the miserable subjected beings we were into friends, sons, collaborators, gods.

For as Augustine himself stated: "God became man so that man could become God." This statement is so true, so consonant with Augustine's own experience that a few lines later he makes this further prodigious statement, so full of poetry and wisdom: "By attaching myself to You with the whole of my being, my life will become living because it is filled with You." So it is in God, whom Augustine calls in his *Confessions* 'Vita vitarum' – 'Life of our life' – that our life becomes living and finds its plenitude.

All the weird suppositions, then, about dependency, enslavement, domination and despotism become meaningless in the light of this quintessentially Christian experience. The Christian does not approach God as though he were a stranger; he approaches God as though he were drawing closer to his own self.

What do you look for in human love? What do you hope to find in it? Exactly what has been described: to find yourself in communion with another being who is interior to yourself and through whom you realise and perfect your interiority.

Well, God is complete Interiority. He has no exterior being. All he can do, then, is to draw us to the inside, establish us in the most intimate reaches of our own self and of a freedom which is inviolable, since in this total intimacy with ourselves there is no alternative but to acknowledge it and help it to grow. This is because God has no other purpose for us than to establish this interiority, to safeguard it and help it to mature. God can never act on us from the outside. He can only activate us from within, penetrating our being without violating our selfhood, yet at the same time effacing the boundaries encircling us to open up a vast space in which we can become what He is: Generosity, Light, Love.

That is why we can say that the world, the universe, the whole of creation is circumscribed by the fragility of God, like the thinking reed. Is there anything more fragile than a reed? But the thinking reed is the arbiter of the world. God appears to us now as one who invites us to become an inviolable liberty, putting Himself in our hands. And we have the terrible power to say 'No', just as we have the power to say 'Yes'.

This is what we read in the Prologue to St John's Gospel: "The light shineth in the darkness, and the darkness comprehended it not. He was in the world, and the world knew Him not. He came into his own and his own received Him not." (Jn. 1: 5, 10, 11)

God was always already there: "You were with me, but I was not with you." He is always already there, but if we are not there it is as though He were non-existent. The greatest love is powerless against a mind which is closed in on itself, refuses to yield. The greatest beauty, the finest music is powerless to open ears that remain stubbornly closed.

God, then, can be defeated. That is why He is a crucified God, crucified by all our refusals to show Him our love, so rendering his Presence powerless, as is made clear by St Augustine: "You were with me, but I was not with You."

The whole world is suspended by a thread to this divine fragility, Love, which can be crushed, rejected, crucified by any one of us. The world, then, is not what we supposed. We have to carry it in our turn, transform it, confer on it its true meaning. We have to bring it into the circle of light and love which will seal the gold ring of our eternal engagement.

It is important, then, to hold on to these three statements of Augustine:

"You were inside, but I was outside." "You were with me, but I was not with You." "By attaching myself to You with my whole being, my life will be living because it is filled with You."

By reflecting on Augustine's amazing journey and his words which so perfectly translate his ascent to the Light, it is for each one of us to listen ourselves for the voice calling us from our innermost depths, seeking to draw us inside and make us free and one with Him, a centre, a beginning, a source and origin.

('Le Dieu intérieur', *Your Face My Light,* pp.109-113, extracts.)

***

Echoes and Reflexions: the Written Word

You will remember the inscription which pilgrims to ancient Greece read on the pediment of the temple to Apollo:

Gnoti Scoton
'Know Yourself'

It signified: know yourself as mortal, not as divine.

The great Thinkers interpreted it as an invitation to philosophise. They rightly considered that man's inner life was the sanctuary of the divinity and they inscribed on their soul these words they had read on stone. For that is where the search for life starts, and there is no greater adventure than this quest to discover who you really are and what you are really called.

When you seriously ask yourself this question, you will suddenly realise how full of mystery it is.

The question of who we are eludes us, and each day we discover unexplored regions in ourselves, unknown territories, whole continents adrift, cities rising and falling: an entire universe in perpetual gestation.

And the mystery attaching to our lives – our hopes and dreams, our sufferings and weaknesses, our grandeur and our misery – is true in one way or another of all our fellow humans.

Yet what we experience as a mystery in ourselves we make light of in others, whilst still professing to know them; we flatter ourselves on our ability to penetrate their psychology, to know them through and through, and we sum them up in two or three character traits which hold the secret of their conduct and personality. We quickly come to identify them with the job they do or the function they carry out and continually pass judgments on them which, if they were turned against ourselves, we would consider to be the height of absurdity, an outrage and an injustice.

So it is that without any pangs of conscience on our part, we negate their souls.

And what is true of those close to us – our children or colleagues or bosses or subordinates – is even truer of human groupings into which we artificially categorise people.

How urgent it is to rid ourselves of this instinct to homogenise, and to recognise that any group is made up of persons, individuals, who each have the duty and inviolable right to live as human beings!

Humanity is in peril of death because all of its problems – whether educational, economic, social or political – are posed in the abstract without any reference to the fundamental question informing them all:

What is man?

What is it we want to save, to preserve in humanity? What is the one fundamental value common to all, on which everything else depends and which we want to safeguard?

It is life, life with its spiritual dignity, that mysterious inner reality without which life is nothing.

(*The Interior Gospel*, op.cit., 2007 (1936), pp.15-19, extracts.)

6. The Adventure of Personhood: Passing from 'Something' to 'Someone'

The theme of interiority of the previous chapter is developed in this one by reference more specifically to St Francis, the second great presence in Zundel's life and a major foundation stone of his theology. Whilst a more accessible saint, perhaps, for the 'ordinary' Christian, in the sense that he did not live an enclosed monastic life but mingled with the people in the highways and byways where the model of poverty and charity he embodied was evident for all to see, the reality for Zundel went much deeper. Through St Francis, poverty assumed for him a more complex metaphysical meaning. It is fundamental to the idea of finding one's true self ('le moi') and becoming Someone, a Person, in the Christian, Zundelian, sense of one who can live out the message of the Gospel – love in the sense of self-giving, total surrender of oneself to the 'other' – unopposed by the egoistic instincts of the 'prefabricated' self and retaining nothing of this self. The way is thus cleared for the emergence of one's originary being conceived in the image of God – the 'rebirth' preached by Christ to Nicodemus, as recurrent a reference in Zundel's theology as Christ's encounter with the Samaritan woman. An abstruse, perhaps superhuman idea for the so-called 'ordinary' Christian, the ideal is validated by the background facts of Francis's early life, like Augustine's tarnished by the same passions as those ruling 'everyman' until, that is, the moment of lucidity or conversion when he embarked on a different course, one dedicated to the ideal of self-oblation.

Abstruse to us ordinary mortals, then, yes, the nature of their 'becoming', of their emergence as 'Persons' may seem. But are not the seeds of the same vocation, the same urge to pursue an inner direction at variance with the world's promptings, experienced intermittently by any number of people who have felt themselves uplifted, purified, inwardly liberated by moments of Grace, epiphanies, which leave them dissatisfied with the parameters of their normal life? "To God all things are possible," the Scriptures say (Mt 19:26). How much more so, Zundel would add, as regards the desire to follow the movements of the spirit where it would lead, if there is the willing collaboration of the individual to become source, origin and creator of himself. Is the individual ever alone if he responds to the challenge? Even though Zundel was humble enough to admit the ultimate is not achievable in life, he himself never renounced the way of perfectibility.

This leads to another original, perhaps provocative notion in Zundel fundamental to Christian doctrine: that of 'le mal', the connotations of which seem so much wider in French. Neither 'sin' nor 'suffering' nor 'evil' seem quite appropriate; perhaps one can only come to it via antithesis, as signifying the opposite to the Good. An essential dimension of 'le mal', for Zundel, is precisely the rejection of the vocation to become Someone and approach that state of inward transparency with God which is the road to human unity, or, as he states in the text, to entering into 'the splendour of our humanity'.

This chapter carries us one step further in Zundel's theology into what we may term the mystique of the human trinity as reflecting this 'splendour', and corresponding to the Divine Trinity, described by Zundel as the 'circumincession' of Father, Son, and Holy Spirit – an eternal, circuitous movement of disappropriation or self-giving between three persons, originating in God as an all-embracing impulse of Love. In human terms, it becomes that state of transparency or authentic communication between the self and the 'other' achieved via unity with the God 'inside' of one, which sets in motion an unending chain of inter-personal relations defined by Love. Rublev's icon of the Trinity is an eloquent biblical image of this eternal God-inspirited élan towards the other. A more scientific mind might conceive of the emergence of the 'person' into this new sphere of being (the 'new birth' in Zundelian terminology) as an original circle of communication turning on an ever-increasing number of axes as it works towards the perfect, all-embracing sphere of Heaven.

The chapter is in two parts, combining the larger parts of two interrelated sermons, the first part dealing with the spiritual ideas outlined above, the second dealing on a more practical, down-to-earth plane with the representative attitude to faith of the 'ordinary' Christian and the change of consciousness required in order to embark on the adventure of Personhood.

***

I

Poverty or Dispossession of Self

The greatest writers are those who with the simplest words can say things of eternal significance.

One of these great sayings was Flaubert's statement: "Why aspire to be something when one can be someone?" The words came into his mind when the poet Baudelaire urged him to support his candidature to the French Academy. Flaubert, scandalised at the thought that a poet could desire any other reward than Beauty, his life's mission, wrote the saying down in his journal.

Passing from something to someone sums up the whole problem of man. We speak a lot about evolution and the mystery of man's origins: Where does he come from? Where does life originate? Is it sparked off by an electrical discharge, a cloud of gas? Does it have a vegetable, mineral or animal source?

That is all very interesting; but isn't the crucial question rather: What are we ourselves going to do with our life? For really, the only interesting thing about our being in the world is that we are free to make choices. Yet we know through experience that catastrophe is often the end result. It rarely happens that the individual becomes 'someone'. Most of the time he is 'something', simply a fragment of the universe, a moment of the species, determined by his race, the continent on which he lives, the colour of his skin, the prejudices of his milieu; and when he loses control of himself, he is worse than an animal. There is nothing as terrible as man's cruelty to man.

It is obvious, then, that whatever explanation we give of evolution, it does not automatically mean we pass from being something to being someone. For that process to take place we have to assume individual responsibility. That is our vocation, the privilege we are born with, together with the giving of ourselves to others, which is the highest form of human grandeur and dignity.

But it remains as such only a possibility. The process does not happen of itself; in addition, it is extremely difficult. In fact, one can virtually say it is impossible, unless one has encountered God as a living reality in one's life.

And here we must not be taken in by the power of the human mind. Our reasoning faculty is not as yet what makes us into humans. For we argue endlessly just to defend our strongly held feelings and points of view. And we know that people can be brainwashed, deprived of their reason, in order to make them confess to ideas which previously they rejected from the depth of their being.

Even though the mind can be put to any number of uses, it is quite separate from the spirit; for the essence of the spirit lies in giving, but in order to operate as such it has to meet someone it can give to. And because the vast majority of people do not find someone they can give to, they never realise this promotion of themselves from something to someone.

This idea can be clarified by reference to St. Francis. Of all the Christian saints, Francis of Assisi is one of the greatest, one of the most extraordinary, one of the most magnificent; he is one of those whose influence is still powerfully felt today because he encountered God in the form of divine poverty.

What a transformation in a man who was all ambition, avid for public recognition and a place in the history books, determined to forge his way out of the bourgeois and merchant class of his origins and become a lord, prince and conqueror, dreaming of dazzling ladies in brilliant tournaments? It was this very same man who came to know the unbounded generosity of God under the name of Dame Poverty, whom he recognised as the True God.

So we see him represented in sackcloth with a girdle round his waist, begging for food or working with peasants in the fields, delighting in a dry crust of bread or water cupped from a spring. It was he, Francis, who before anyone else penetrated to the true depths of the Trinity and through the light emanating from him revealed its meaning to us: God, the very opposite of a self-regarding, self-admiring entity, gives up everything of Himself, is pure communication, a Person, Someone who surrenders Himself in an eternal process of giving.

It was St. Francis who gave us the understanding that life in its highest human form is a life of giving, of charity, of self-dispossession, of love. It is the happiness expressed in the first of the Beatitudes – "Happy are the poor in spirit" (Mt 5:3) – the joy in life of giving up all one has. God is God because He has nothing: divinity belongs to no one; it is the Father looking to the Son and the Son looking to the Father in the unity and embrace of the Holy Spirit. This is how we are drawn into the intimacy of God's heart and the revelation that the meaning of existence lies in a total giving of ourselves, for we have come face to face with 'Someone' – or rather felt the presence of Someone inside of ourselves – to give ourselves to, One who has never ceased to offer Himself to us in love and to seek a place in our hearts, a God who has never ceased, in a word, to give Himself to us.

And this opens up a totally new perspective! If the process is to continue, it cannot do so automatically, of itself. It is we who have to make it happen, and that is precisely where our vocation as human beings lies. We are called to be a focus for all the energies that are at work in the universe, to put a face on them and help them to reach their plenitude by turning them into an offering of light and love. It is when we do this that we change from being something into being someone.

It is a mission of the highest dignity and honour, one in which we must take the greatest pride, an adventure that Christ placed at the very centre of our vocation through baptism. We have to turn the world from the blind, mechanistic forces of darkness, fatality and determinism carrying it, which lurk everywhere in the natural sphere, and bring it into the sphere of liberty, charity, generosity and love.

And this is where we realise that it is totally impossible for those who have not encountered God as a living presence within themselves and realised through Him that existence is synonymous with giving... It is impossible for such people as these, who have not received the Gospel of Divine Poverty, to realise their human vocation.

For to be truly human, to be someone, is only possible for the person who can centre his whole being, draw all the fibres of his being into an offering to eternal Love...as too to all those fellow humans who are unaware they carry God within them, where he is waiting for us too, just as He is waiting for us in the depths of our own self.

This process, we may note, often takes place amidst the most humble in society. Think of all those women, unknown factory workers and others, whose names will never go down in history, but somewhere, toiling away in a back kitchen, they have made the supreme sacrifice of themselves, achieving in the manner of St. Francis the highest that humankind can achieve. And here we are not talking of book learning, of technical skill, of being clever and important in the eyes of the world. We are talking of a silent vocation, of a call which is heard deep down in the heart and is responded to in a silent act of giving.

Just as God's greatness resides exclusively in Love and an eternal process of disappropriation, dispossession of Himself, human greatness too resides in a private act of self-giving, often taking place far away from the public gaze. It casts a magnificent radiance which traverses frontiers and oceans to touch the whole of humanity in that mysterious circuit of the communion of Saints in which 'every soul that elevates itself, elevates the world' (Elisabeth Lesuer).

The essential point to be retained, as regards this unique, overwhelming appearance of St. Francis in the history of Christianity, is the question of what we are going to do with the life which has come down to us, wherever it has come from, this life which offers us the freedom to choose, to go beyond ourselves, to give of ourselves to others.

God is there ready to help us to embark on this silent, heroic adventure, learning each day more effectively to give of ourselves through the small things that make up the fabric of our daily lives, bringing to others in so far as we are able the light of an open, friendly face. For the finest revelation of God's love and the best way of bringing those around us to the greatness of self-giving is to bring into the environment in which we live the smile of God's Goodness.

This is what saves the human being from despair: when he is no longer confronted by a blank wall but by a face which is the face of someone, a person with a heart, a smile of friendship, the breath of sympathy and understanding; and he begins to understand that he is not alone and abandoned in the universe, just a thing in the midst of a world of things. There is the breath of creativity in him, the call of a new person to an adventure which is infinite.

('Passer de quelque chose à quelqu'un', *Your Face My Light*, pp.57-61.)

II

Still the Pharisee: The Self as Obstacle

What immediately strikes one in the story of Christ as recounted in the Gospels is that Christ's enemies are all very respectable people. Almost all of them are people of standing: local governors, high priests, theologians, interpreters, specialists on the Bible, experts on the Law. In a word, then, they are highly respectable people.

So respectable, in fact, that they go further than the Law demands, like the Pharisees, for fear of not respecting all the details of the law. It is their way of reassuring themselves that they have done everything God requires of them, more in fact, so they have nothing to reproach themselves for.

These are the people who most vehemently opposed the activity of Christ, who passed for the friend of the poor, of publicans, sinners and women of shady morals, and who was frowned upon as such by the powers that be in the Church and theological hierarchy of the time.

The question we need to ask ourselves is whether it is not still the same today. Isn't the way of life of the Pharisees still the prevailing characteristic of the Christianity we live by? But let's be clear what we mean by the term. When we speak of Pharisees we must not immediately think of the parable of the Pharisee and the publican, where the Pharisee is the man full of his own self-importance, the hypocrite, who is always asserting his superiority over others. That is not the meaning of the term used here. The word 'Pharisee' is being used rather to denote a school of theologians distinguished by its extreme devotion to the Law and to the service of God.

How could it come about, then, that these well-meaning people – as far at least as they were able – instinctively found themselves in the opposing camp to Jesus Christ? The reason is that Christ contained within Him the seeds of revolution, a revolution in the conception of God and a revolution in the conception of man, and, following on from that, a revolution in the conception of the idea of the 'Good'.

It is because we have failed to understand the revolution instigated by Christ that we ourselves have remained Pharisees. For it is abundantly clear that the moral outlook of Christians as a whole is that of the Pharisees at the time of Christ, focused on good works, right thinking, upright living, presenting an unblemished face to the world, concentrating all their efforts on maintaining an honourable reputation which gained people's respect and confidence.

There is nothing we can say. The vast majority of Christians, Pharisees in the sense outlined, are well-meaning as such and people of the utmost good faith, for they have not learned anything different. What, then, should they have learned? Exactly what we discover when we put our own selves under scrutiny: that evil [the opposite of good] is our own 'self', the possessive, proprietorial self which takes everything for itself, including credit for the good works it has performed, thus cancelling out the good it has done by the good it has failed to become.

And there lies the key to the great revolution instigated by Jesus. It is not a question of 'doing things' but of 'becoming someone', a person who is a source, a space, an agency of liberty.

If we look at ourselves more closely, we will see that under our honest exterior which makes us pass for respectable citizens, there are all sorts of bad feelings lurking deep down inside of us: the will to vengeance and one-upmanship, rivalries, resentments, hostility, old unsettled scores flaring up again, death wishes, pleasure in the sufferings of others. These thoughts may not be conscious, deliberately intended, for they belong rather to our primitive self, the remains of which we have never fully shaken off. And that, really, is what we are, primitive, uncultivated beings, precisely because we have not undergone a radical transformation of ourselves. Our virtues are like those of the Pharisees, peacock feathers inserted into the plumage of hens and ducks, that is to say, they are not rooted in our true self. So after doing everything possible to maintain a facade in front of others, we crumble when the true test comes, and we find a way of betraying our finest intentions whilst still seeking to maintain the surface picture.

In saying these things I am not seeking to accuse anybody in particular; for I admit to being the first person guilty. I am simply trying to convey the amazing originality of the morality of the Gospels, so that we can at last accede to the marvellous Kingdom of Divine Liberty which is our calling.

We need, then, to pay attention when we use the terms 'I' and 'me' and ask ourselves who this 'I' and 'me' are. The answer may be 'no-one', for we are still stuck in our infantile self. When we first started saying 'I' and 'me', we were children. Who did the terms refer to? To what we were then, is the answer, that is to say, to a child cast into existence by a heredity not chosen by him, a being, therefore, who is purely a result, a bundle of needs and determinisms. And instead of using the personal pronouns 'I' and 'me' to signify what they should – an original creative power – we continue through life to use them in relation to the infantile being we still are, vehemently defending something which is not us. And this points to a very important truth; it is that our self-infatuation is our prison, a prison in which we suffocate ourselves because we are the first to say no to our own liberty. And this is true of the most talented people; for intelligence does not come into the question.

Only the saints escape this force of determinism. They alone nurture their being as a space of light and liberty and openness, to which anyone may come to breathe of the air into which they were born.

This is the Good we have to become: a being which has broken free of its infantile self and is now capable of bringing a new dimension into the world in its capacity as source, origin and creator.

In embracing this true morality of Christ, which found itself up against the whole barrage of pharisaism, we have to start off by realizing that the entire construction of 'I' and 'me' to which we are so viscerally attached means absolutely nothing. And if we go right through with the idea we will be in a position to enter through what Jesus calls 'the new birth' into the splendour of our humanity. For as soon as we have disconnected ourselves from the self which is not ourself, we will feel God's heartbeat in our own and the longed-for Presence of the Holy Spirit.

('Se libérer de soi', *Your Face My Light*, pp.175-180, extracts.)

***

Echoes and Reflexions: The Written Word

The human condition can be summed up in this formula, which is the supreme truth for me: I do not exist, but I can exist… Our being lies in the possibility of being.

Nothing is more important and more difficult than to let our whole being be permeated by the light of an invisible Reality which we seek to experience as the Light of our Life…

Liberty presupposes a permanent effort to liberate ourselves; dignity presupposes a permanent effort to become the inviolable sanctuary of an infinite Presence; responsibility presupposes an unceasing commitment to our mission as creators; immortality presupposes developing the capacity to carry ourselves rather than letting the universe carry us; finally, being a person presupposes that we transform ourselves into a universal good that can enrich the world, liberating the whole of creation which groans in travail, in the words of St Paul. If we use these high-sounding words but do not live them out in practice, human misery, incapable of hot air, will go on increasing…

Wonderment is that privileged moment when we awaken to a new dimension in ourselves and are momentarily cured of ourselves and transported into a Presence – we do not need to name it – which gives us a complete sense of self-realisation at the same time as delivering us from ourselves…

Our primitive, prefabricated self draws a veil over our 'possibility of being' and turns us away from self-realisation. It follows, therefore, that we have to start by liberating ourselves from this 'me' which is the focus of everything that enslaves us...

The 'starred hours', as they are called by Zweig, those hours of wonderment, love or compassion when we are cured of ourselves and suddenly lose sight of ourselves to focus our gaze on Another – who appears to us in a spectacle of nature, a scientific discovery, a piece of music, or the look on a person's face – are hours of grace which open up the way for us. In their light our search for a deeper sense of being takes on meaning; the emptiness in us is ready to be filled... We become, as it were, our own creator, but in the form of an offering of love which frees us from our self and receives us into a Love which is infinite.

(*I is another [Je est un autre]*, Ed. Anne Sigier, 1997 [1971], pp. 8 and 53, 138, 58, 18, 55-56.)

7. A Living Cathedral and Icon:
Your Face My Light

The preceding chapters have led, progressively, to the great climax of Zundelian spirituality: achieving 'the splendour of our humanity'. This means nothing less, however evanescent the experience, than knowing eternity in this life, achieving divinity on earth (cf. 'God became man so that man might become God'). How render this truth accessible? The problem of expressing the ineffable, whether in God or in man, in order to communicate ever more clearly the 'interior gospel', was one which had preoccupied Zundel from the beginning. However convinced he was of the limitations of language to express the ultimate of human experience, Zundel was endowed with a singular gift, like St John of the Cross. It was that of poetry, his musicality and lyricism carrying one at times almost on a wave of mysticism, creating the atmosphere of another world. Like all poets, when ordinary language failed he had recourse to metaphor. Two in particular, through their rich associations spiritually across the ages and across cultures, illumine his texts: these are the cathedral and the icon, symbols which go to the very essence of his vision of the 'person' and are poetically enriched from sermon to sermon.

This final chapter includes extracts from three interrelated sermons incorporating these metaphors, each one focusing individually at the same time on a specific aspect of Zundel's theology as a whole. The first one, 'Presence of the Body', developing Paul's affirmation that the body is the 'temple of the Holy Spirit', equates the idea of 'self-creation' (the third element of Zundel's Trinitarian call to the individual to be 'source, origin, and creator') with the progressive glorification of the body as the agency of interior communion with the other in the mystical unification of Humanity. The human face is the focal point of this revelatory power, radiating its inner light. The second extract illustrates the liturgical dimension of the image by reference to the 'mystical body of the Eucharist'. The third takes us into the core Zundelian theme of God as Mother, identifying the Face with the supreme attribute of maternal tenderness and Love. 'Giving' or 'self-giving' ('le don' in Zundelian terminology) achieves its full expressive power through the iconic splendour of the Face, or as it is expressed in the title of this piece, 'the transparency of the look, source and fruit of love'.

The Face once seen, made real by reference to the perennial memory of mother and infant child wrapped in each other's gaze, becomes like other 'starred hours' – but none more potently than this –the focus of contemplation as a force for 're-animation' of the transcendent within one.

***

I

'Presence of the Body'

I wish you could be a priest for a moment, administering Communion. I know few spectacles more moving and magnificent than these human faces lost in devotion, reaching out to the Divine Presence, there waiting. The human being rarely displays such nobility and grandeur! I never administer Communion without being filled with wonder at the power of the human face to express the infinite.

Yes, it is true: the human body has the power to express the infinite, to reflect God's radiance, to focus on a single point which is the seat of the eternal Presence.

St Paul reminds us that we are the temple of God (1 Co 3:16), the members of Jesus Christ (1 Co 12:12); together we are His Mystical Body (Rm 12:5), thus members one of another. There is, therefore, in our body which is our own self this expressive power capable at one and the same time of concealing our secret from those not worthy of knowing it and of revealing it to those who are interior to ourselves.

That is why the New Testament already glorifies our bodies here in our earthly life and commits us to bringing them into the sphere of eternity by treating them as the temple of God. There lies the wonder of wonders. *All the cathedrals in the world are nothing compared with the cathedral of our own self,*[37] which is the true residence of God where He seeks to communicate His presence. So much so that our body, perceived and experienced as a vocation of liberation and the sacrament of an eternal Presence, strikes us as being the ultimate, most effective Gospel of all.

As our presence in the world is normally registered through the history of our body, God's Presence too can only be inscribed in history and become a concrete element of human life *through the agency of the face which radiates the Divine Presence.*[38]

Could one make any more wonderful, momentous statement than this: the only convincing gospel, the only one that can make us alive to God's presence, is our face rapt in silent contemplation, transparent to the other, emitting to the world a sort of unique melody which reflects the singularity of our own person and collaborates in this unique way in the revelation of God? Each one of us has received a feature of His Infinite Face, to manifest it to the world, and this revelation which is our very being and purpose in life can be made by us alone.

It is only when we see our body as the repository of all these riches of expression and evangelisation, and of all the mysteries attached to God's presence, that we will appreciate the full importance of treating our bodies as the greatest cathedral of all, the living, eternal sanctuary of God.

---

[37] Italics are mine.
[38] Ibid.

II

'The Mystical Body of the Eucharist'

Oh, divine Liturgy of the Mass! If we lived it, we would be radically transformed! For we would live the whole of Humanity, the whole of History, we would bring together in the love we feel all the faces, known or unknown, who have left a trace, or who have not left one, in the History of Man.

And the whole of today's world, this world of blood and tears, of violence and dispute, would be illumined by the reality of God's presence within us. To live Mass is to become a vast inner space of silence in which all extraneous noises are suppressed so as to hear God's heart beating within us, waiting to communicate itself, through us, to the whole universe.

And as we look at the lamp of the Tabernacle and are attuned by its silence to the silence of Christ who is in our midst, we cannot fail to be drawn into the depths of God's presence and to feel that we ourselves have become a living cathedral, and that it is in the tabernacle of our own selves that Christ aspires to communicate Himself to the world.

('Eucharistie et corps mystique', *Your Face My Light*, pp.462-463, extracts.)

III

'The Transparency of the Look, Source and Fruit of Love'

Maternal love shows us that to understand another person, to really know them and see all they are capable of achieving in life and help them to achieve it, you have to love that person and be in tune with them; you have to know them from the inside. That is why it is difficult for most people to really get to know each other: love is missing. They see each other from the outside, in terms of their function, their job, their profession. They see each other as objects rather than as persons endowed with infinite dignity and value.

Sartre made the terrible assertion that each person's look violates the space of the other. For each of us considers ourselves to be the centre of the universe, and others appear to us to be circulating in territory that belongs to us. When we look out into the street, we see houses and men and women passing by. But we do not experience them as people like us, full of an infinite mystery. They are simply people to be looked at, a part of the scenery; they are denied existence by the other person's look, reduced to the state of objects.

If, then, to know another human being we need new eyes which confer on them unbounded respect and bring out the best in them, restoring them to a sense of hope and belief in an infinite Love, how much more, when it is a question of coming to know God, do we need an open, transparent heart and the offering of a life illumined by love. Otherwise, we will just take God to ourselves and turn Him into an idol.

That is where the difficulty lies. If we are such mediocre Christians who submit to every sort of distraction and fail to see God as a living person who draws us to Him, strangers to the passion for God of a St Francis or John of the Cross, it is because the eyes of our spirit are closed and the ears of our heart are deaf and our life is not transparent to the Divine Light.

There is, in fact, the same distance between ourselves and our true being as between ourselves and God. We imagine that God is far away from us. It is we who are absent from ourselves. It is because we have not found our true self so as to know who we are and realise our vocation as living beings that we do not know God. Or we simply know Him from the outside, like the people we see in the street who are simply a part of the landscape, the scenery.

We have to change the way we look and the way we feel, as is demonstrated so wonderfully by St Augustine in the account of his conversion... Our situation is that of beings on the outside, outside of our own selves. We live on the surface of existence and of the world, and that is why, strangers to ourselves, we are strangers to God... Augustine recognised that the moment he entered into the intimacy of his own being and found himself was the moment he discovered someone waiting there for him, eternally waiting.

And it was at this very moment of encounter with God and with himself that he was delivered from enslavement to the things of the world and to the play of his passions, and was plunged into the unbounded space of his own liberty...to become a source, an origin, a creator, a person, a value, a treasure that would never diminish, never die.

The only revelation of God is man. God can only reveal Himself via a human life which has become transparent to Him, for true knowledge of a person comes through reciprocal love – just as the mother knows her child through the love that she bears him and the child knows its mother through the love it feels in return for her. Just as people can only know each other via the light of their inner being, we can only know God through that silent dialogue in which we become ourselves through losing ourselves in Him.

This process of purification is essential. We have to free our own selves in order not to turn God into an idol. If we are often in a state of despair, feeling God's face is far from us and looks on us with hostility, as a stranger, it is because we have not yet been born to the person we truly are; we are still controlled by our glands, our nerves, our moods, our resentments, our state of fatigue or physical deterioration; basically, we are not free.

Do we want to be free? That is the question facing us at every moment of our lives. Do we want to become a space of light and generosity? Do we want to rise above the animal state into which we are born? Do we want to become a source springing up into eternal life, as Jesus put it to the Samaritan woman? Do we want to bring to God a truly open, transparent heart, and a diaphanous look no longer bound by appearances, and the joyous exhilaration of coming into the orbit of Eternal Beauty?

That is the gift offered to us by God and which we desire of Him. Freedom! The Christian vocation is precisely that: to be free, a slave to nothing, limitless in aspiration, conferring on everything we encounter in life an infinite dimension and value; it is to transform the whole of one's existence into a space of light and a pulsation of love. It is in so far as we make this our calling that God will cease to be an idol, and His Face will appear before us each morning entirely new, a Face as yet unknown but already known, a Face which can stir only joy and wonderment in us, for God is the source of all music, of all poetry, of all love, and of all beauty.

So we, like Augustine, will no longer wish to be outside. We will wish to focus all our attention inside. And enveloped by God's light, educated by His look, we will develop a new look ourselves to project upon people and the world, and life will be transfigured, clothed in beauty.

('La transparence du regard, source et fruit de l'amour', *Your Face My Light*, pp.329-333, extracts.)

***

Echoes and Reflexions: the written word

These final 'Echoes and Reflexions' are taken from Zundel's first book (Poem of the Holy Liturgy) and his last, (What man and what God) in the interests of conveying the unity and coherence of his vision.

Isn't the first church we have to create the invisible cathedral constructed in our own hearts to the silent Word? (*Poem of the Holy Liturgy*, op.cit., p.109.)

If we each give ourselves with every step we take to the Light which is in us, and if we strive with every fibre of our being to reveal in all our activities, both public and private, and in all our relations both with others and with our own self what we sincerely believe to be the Spiritual point of view,

we will have done all that is asked of us as humans and we will have collaborated in the most effective way possible in the coming of God's Kingdom: 'for God is spirit and they that worship him must worship him in spirit and in truth'.
(Ibid., p.104.)

What is saintliness other than that transparency of the self which is pure self-giving?
(Ibid., p.133.)

***

The cathedral is the habitation of a morsel of bread. It survives through time because of this bread, the luminous point to which its forest of pillars leads; and conversely, this bread has led to its expansion in space, to the ever-higher thrust of its vaults and the ever-greater resplendence of its stained glass. Eternal life, present here below in the Eucharist – where God's silence happily compensates for all our noisiness as humans – has brought into being, through faith nurtured over time, this immense vessel of stone which has set sail for eternity. Eternity is present to us in this symbol which expresses in material terms the ultimate dimension of our earthly adventure, transfigured in the form of a spiritual élan located in the most secret parts of our sensibility.
(*What Man and What God, [Quel homme et quel Dieu]*, Paris, Ed. Saint Augustin, 1997, p.128.)

Epilogue
The Gospel of Man, Eternity on Earth

There is something so unique, so fantastic, so crazy even about the Religion of Man – this universal religion which excludes no-one, is available to all and carried by all. When one looks at man and his miserable condition, man bound by envy and greed, using his greatest discoveries to the end of destruction, what is it about him that deserves this credit accorded him? The answer is that it is precisely this 'credit' of divine generosity which bit by bit should lead him to himself and the aspiration to the infinite inside of him, calling him to dedicate his entire life and being to the pursuit and demonstration of it. That sums it up. If one doesn't believe in Man, it is impossible to believe in God.

But God can only offer Himself to us; He can never force Himself on us, and that is why he seems so often to be absent. But it is we ourselves who are absent. Once we are present the Kingdom of God will be revealed, Truth will illuminate the world, Music will be heard in the silence of our hearts, Love will form a chain of happiness and human fraternity will be realised.

This, then, is our vocation: to identify with others, to take on our shoulders the sufferings and the hope of the world, and starting right now, at home, in the office, in the work-place: to 'give credit' to those around us and enlighten them with the symbol of washing the disciples' feet, to be attentive to the hidden life within them and become for them the space where liberty breathes freely. So they will realise that Heaven is not up there behind the clouds, but is here, now, in the secret recesses of our own heart.

('The Religion of Man', *Your Face My Light*, pp.152-155, extracts.)

It is not a question of dying but of not dying, of triumphing over death today by letting our bodies breathe the Divine Presence within us, hidden like an invisible sun in the deepest part of our being.

('Conquering Death in Life', *Your Face My Light,* p.261, extract.)

'We were there just as on other days, doing the same things, expressing the same attitudes, and this light suddenly flows past us, revealing beyond the stultifying routine of our days the sense of a Presence, still obscure but recognisable in the emotion we feel. It is like dawn lighting up a cathedral nave, gradually illuminating the glass of the windows with a diaphanous light which reveals a heavenly choir singing the Canticle to the Sun.'

(*The Interior Gospel*, p.138)

Bibliography

The main source used for translations from Zundel is *Ton visage ma lumière, 90 sermons inédits de Maurice Zundel*, collated by Bernard de Boissière, Paris, Desclée, 1989.

Other key sources for both his life and his work are:

Maurice Zundel, by Bernard de Boissière and France-Marie Chauvelot, Paris, Presses de la Renaisssance, 2004.

Présence de Maurice Zundel, Bulletin des Amis de Maurice Zundel (AMZ France), 4 issues per year; to date 109 issues published.

Books by Zundel quoted / referred to (listed according to chronological completion)

Le Poème de la Sainte Liturgie, Paris, Desclée, 1998; (original publication, Ed. St Augustin, 1926).

Le Mystère de la connaissance, (unpublished, 1932).

L'Evangile intérieur, Saint-Maurice / Paris, Ed. St Augustin, 2007; (original publication 1936).

Ouvertures sur le vrai, Paris, Desclée, 1989; (completed 1940).

L'Homme passe l'homme, Itinéraire, Ed. du Jubilé, 2005; (first published 1948).

La Beauté du monde entre ses mains, Québec, Ed. Anne Sigier, 2004; (collection of articles published between 1927 and 1950).

Croyez-vous en l'homme, Paris, Ed. du Cerf, 2008; (completed 1955).

Hymne à la joie, Québec, Ed. Anne Sigier, 1992; (original publication, Ed. Ouvrières, 1965).

Je est un autre, Québec, Ed. Anne Sigier, 1997; (completed 1971).

Quel homme et quel Dieu, Saint-Maurice, Ed. St Augustin, 1997.

Other books by Zundel which inform the text

Recherche de la personne, Paris, Desclée, 1990; (completed 1938).

Allusions (Présentations par Bernard de Boissière, André Girard, Marc Donzé), Ed. Anne Sigier / Cerf / St Augustin, 2007; (original publication, Cairo, 1941).

Avec Dieu dans le quotidien, Ed. Saint Maurice (Suisse) / St Augustin, 1997; (retreat articles 1953, presented by Marc Donzé).

Silence, Parole de vie, Québec, Ed. Anne Sigier, 1990; (retreat articles, 1959).

Morale et mystique, Québec, Ed. Anne Sigier, 1999; (original publication, Desclée, 1962).

La Vérité, source unique de liberté, Québec, Ed. Anne Sigier, 2001; (articles published between 1965 and 1971).

Ta Parole comme une source, 85 sermons inédits de Maurice Zundel, Québec, Ed. Anne Sigier, 1987.

L'Homme, le grand malentendu, (collection 'Vivre l'Evangile avec Maurice Zundel', presented by André Girard), Versailles, Ed. Saint Paul, 2007.

Books about Maurice Zundel

(Editor Marc Donzé), *Regards croisés sur Maurice Zundel*, Proceedings of colloquium held at Neuchâtel on centenary of Zundel's birth, Ed. St Augustin / Cerf, 1997.

François Rouiller, *Le Scandale du mal et de la souffrance chez Maurice Zundel*, Saint Maurice, Ed. St Augustin, 2002.

France-Marie Chauvelot, *Maurice Zundel, Vivre Dieu : L'art et la joie de croire*, (based on extracts from Zundel's work), Paris, Presses de la Renaissance, 2007.

France du Guérand (with Maurice Zundel), *A l'Ecoute du silence*, Paris, Pierre Téqui, 2011.

Bernard de Boissière (in collaboration with France-Marie Chauvelot), *Avec Maurice Zundel, Mes Heures Etoilées*, Paris, Ed. Salvator, 2012.

Background sources / references (listed according to their occurrence in text)

Richard Harries, *Art and the Beauty of God*, London, Mowbray, 1993.

Victor Hugo, *Les Misérables*, Penguin.

John Russell, *Switzerland*, London, Batsford, 1962.

Walter Weideli, *Moine aujourd'hui*, Paris, Ed. du Cerf, 1986.

François Cheng, *Assisi,* Paris, Albin Michel, 2015.

Charles Du Bos, *Qu'est-ce que la littérature ?* Paris, Ed. L'Age d'Homme, 1989.

Thomas Browne, *Religio Medici*, 1635, Everyman edition.

Karen Armstrong, *Mohammed, a Biography of the Prophet,* London, Victor Gollancz, 1991.

St Augustine, *Confessions*, Penguin edition.

François Mauriac, *Mes grands hommes*, Paris, Ed. du Rocher, 1949.